Loneliness is Lovely

MEENA OM

ISBN 979-8-89632-355-6

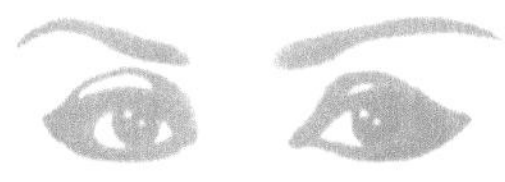

Pranam

Gratitude

Love

And Salutations

To All

Who have firmly resolved to

transform absolutely and are dedicated to

Mana Marg — the infallible path of Pranam

based on Truth Love Karm and Light.

Compilation - Mahika and Anubhuti

Pranam

The truth is here. Let us join hands to be part of the Pranam

Movement

To awaken Bharat to its true spiritual potential

To merge Ved and Vigyan, Vidya and Gyan

To experience the Anand of being human

A movement dedicated to establishing Nature's Law of truth

love karm and light by the spiritual realisation of the ever-evolving

Universal Consciousness.

We aspire for absolute transformation – spiritual, social, political and

economic, based on the guidance of the eternal truth of Nature's Law.

CONTENTS

Contents

PREFACE

Throughout years of interacting with seekers, one topic surfaces repeatedly: loneliness. Some seek reasons for their solitary existence, while others yearn for deliverance from a life burdened by apathy, fear, self-loathing, and despair.

Yet, being alone is entirely natural. The Universe is a tapestry of stars, planets, comets, and asteroids—each existing independently. They relate to one another through gravity or light but maintain an appropriate distance, straying, fluctuating or drawing to keep their specific individuality intact. Their energy systems are accurately balanced, governed by how much they give and take—a harmony sustained for millennia.

Closer to home, plants and animals may live in groups, yet each remains inherently self-reliant. Separated from their kind, they adapt, surviving without succumbing to self-pity. They act, taking the necessary steps to reconnect or thrive alone.

Even within our bodies, the cells function as independent universes, reflecting the macrocosm. As the Vedic sutra beautifully states: *Yatha pinde, tatha brahmande* – like body such the Universe. Each cell is complete with all the information, capable of regeneration and thriving in its environment. Consider the embryo: ensconced in the womb, it resides in a state of quiet *samadhi*, or deep dhyan, but receptive to everything required for it's perfect formation until it is ready to face the world.

Uniquely, humans have grown dependent on relationships and energy exchanges, forgetting how to be self-sufficient. This was never the case centuries ago. Our rishi-munis, Vedic seer-scientists were totally one with Nature and could understand her directives, messages and the Universal mechanism. Even as a child of 4 or 5, I remember retreating to my secluded spot to connect with the voice within or just be in intense dhyan. Sometimes my family members would seek me out and try to rouse me, nudging or pinching me if I did not react, but I would remain unmoved, silent and connected. This has been the case till today.

My small eight-by-eight room, where I conduct most of my *sadhna* and trance writings, has witnessed profound moments—astral travels, out-of-body experiences, dhyan, and even 21-day fasts. All this happens when I am silent and totally by myself. My being is usually alone but never lonely.

Traditionally, in Bharat, solitude is neither looked down upon or shunned. It was taken as a phase or a 'happening' in life and sometimes greatly sought after for some intense dhyan, penance or sadhna by true seekers.

When we recognise that such happenings are orchestrated by our innermost divine core for our growth according to our individual traits, they become meaningful. Let these events unfold naturally, like the rhythm of breath or the beating of the heart. Flow with them, staying aware, and extract the best from each experience that is indicating towards some higher plane.

The larger picture always reveals itself in time.

The Supreme Intelligence takes full charge of this mechanism, only our mind is unaware. We need to be open to decode the messages these bring, just like the planet Earth, which is always receptive to all the elements and energies of the Universe, creating a grand symphony of life through them.

It lets life happen, survives and ensures the survival of the fittest – satyam shivam sunderam – truthful benevolent beautiful, according to Supreme Intelligence and Cosmic Design.

Pranam

Meena Om

৪৩৫৪

FOREWORD

A few days ago my daughter excitedly called to say that an anonymous person had paid for her and her friend's dinner. A random act of kindness could generate so much happiness and positivity! But the sad reality is that kindness and empathy are rare and surface occasionally. Empathy in simple words is "to touch the heart of the other," but in this fast paced tech and AI world, where people are into 'selfie culture' and are preferring 'internet bots' as companions, isolation and loneliness is growing.

Therapy and counselling have become the new buzz words and fashion statements! Not just adults, even very young children are being pushed for counselling. Fear, anxiety, stress, depression, frustration, and anger are on the rise. People find themselves stuck in a cycle of repetitive patterns of thoughts and behaviours. Even years of therapy does not help some to break the barriers of hard wired thought patterns and age-old inner tunings…wonder why?

Counsellors and therapists like the medical doctors have to follow a set protocol and while doing so they also carry their own biases. Therapy can provide various tools or coping mechanisms; however, these strategies are usually not permanent solutions to the deep rooted problems, but ways to deal with the reactions of the mind. Counselling encourages the client to use more of their analytical minds, thus mind chatter and mental webs hardly diminish. If none of the simple strategies such as journaling, setting boundaries or mindfulness work, counsellors encourage clients to look at more involved ways such as cognitive behaviour therapy, psychodynamic therapy etc. Sadly, the 'loop' of counselling rarely ends. Rather than going inwards and facing the truth of one's sensitivities and shortcomings at the root level, one is encouraged to look at the outward practices to handle one's conduct and reactions.

Therapy and counselling can be expensive and require consistency along with family support. But there is another way for self-help and self-love, which can bring about metamorphic like effect. Practicing a holistic approach of introspection at the body, mind and soul level can encourage transformation leading to cogent ways of handling various chapters of life.

Loneliness is plaguing one in four people in the world and most of these people are struggling to cope with being 'left alone.' In times like these it is a relief to read *Loneliness is Lovely* as Meena Om has written her truth. She has lived and experienced all that she writes.

Meena ji's simple yet intriguing strategies of writing a daily journal that most therapists also recommend but do not teach the method, for being in tune with the energies of the day and Nature.

Or how to be aware and witness the self in a non-judgemental way to diminish the subconscious baggage of guilt, fear, anxiety etc. She talks about the energy of emotions and negative thoughts that are much needed for positive growth. Her emphasis on the vibrations that the choice of words can create in shaping our environment is important in handling the complexities of life; or how to utilise one's leisure time for character building. The chapter on breathing with awareness can be a cathartic experience. Meena ji's simple thoughts on bringing clarity with dhyan, which is also the need of the hour, will open many vistas for the seeker. And not to miss the chapter on raising one's frequency by connecting with an evolved soul so as to sail through life with ease and peace.

I am extremely humbled and grateful to be graced with writing this foreword for an evolved soul who radiates with the light and the voice of Consciousness. I want to conclude with a short story of a bodhisthva who reached the stage of enlightenment and was asked to seek a boon. He said, "I don't want sovereignty over this Universe or life in the Heavens. But may I attain the perfect enlightenment to release the unreleased, to console the unconsoled and to liberate the unliberated." Meenaji's enlightened words will console the reader and illuminate the path towards the stages of release and liberation.

Pranam Om Om Om

Nisha Kalia Diddi is US based
Educational Diagnostician and
Volunteer Crisis Counsellor

༄༅

I ME MYSELF

I Me Myself

Me, myself, my God

My soul

And

My tranquillity

I am five

I am not alone

This tranquillity is what God loves!

Chapter 2

BEING ALONE

Saroj was in her late 50's when she met me. A reverent, creative soul, who loved to paint 'eyes.' She lived with her family close by and would often come unannounced, tears in her eyes and pain in her heart, struggling to make sense of her life. She felt increasingly neglected, isolated and ignored by her family. Her husband had stopped giving her any attention and would push her to see various doctors for her mental state.

The first time we met, she stayed for more than four hours, crying and desperately seeking help. I could tell that all was not well. Saroj, was a bundle of many spiritual pitfalls, self-pity, self-depreciation and a total lack of purpose. She had spent most of her life raising her children, and now when they were married and settled, she was insignificant to them and Saroj had lost sense of purpose.

She had even attempted suicide a few times. As I held her close, her tears welled up and began to flow copiously. She needed to release all the 'baggage' of insinuations, loathing and neglect that had made her shun the world around her. Slowly, her body relaxed and she lay in surrender.

It is then that I reminded her that she was a talented artist and a loving human being. "Life is beautiful and we are here to make it more beautiful," I said. Nature has never intended us to be forlorn, even if we are alone. The concept of 'loneliness' is alien to our culture. In the yesteryears, the joint family system was a great support. The elders in the family set examples of right thinking and conduct by their actions and often acted as therapists for the younger ones. The younger generation was there to create an energetic atmosphere through their physical actions and liveliness. A sense of belonging, love and care reverberated in the environment. Even at times when someone was alone, there was always something happening in the family like various chores or crafts to practice, whether it was weaving, embroidery or even making pickles! Or the spiritual and motivating talks by the elders that would impart subtle learnings and cultural traditions for all. For those who were spiritually inclined, the quiet time was used for spiritual practices and rituals, enhancing peace and imparting anand – a state that neither represents happiness or sadness, but compete tranquillity and equanimity. Infact, the Bhagwad Geeta also mentions, one of the signs of a spiritually evolved Sadhak is that of one actively seeking solitude and content to being alone.

Saroj followed my suggestions and accepted her state. She worked on her shortcomings to transform her loneliness to blossom as an artist. So she experienced a renewed sense of self-worth, purpose and confidence thus improving her relationships and her standing in her house.

There are many different states of being lonely:

- The first is, being petrified of being alone at any time, nurturing a fear of being left alone or left behind.

- The second, feeling lonely because of lack of companionship.

- The third, finding oneself feeling alone even in a crowd.

- The fourth, actively seeking loneliness and enjoying it as 'me time'.

- And finally, totally comfortable being alone but never lonely – expanded and connected to the whole creation by feeling a part of the cosmic family.

Relating to one or more of the above states defines our relationship with ourselves and reflects the level of our spiritual evolution.

Life has been given to us to realise our true self, but we negate the opportunities, states and opportunities for self-actualisation and being our authentic self in the dazzle and the humdrum of this materialistic world.

Loneliness should be taken as a beautiful phase of life, an occasion for soul searching, a golden chance to reshuffle, redirect our conscious mind to let go and allow the subconscious to surface for releasing all the accumulated heaviness or weight and hinderances in growth. The conscious mind is full of worldly chatter and old tunings, but a clear subconscious allows us to develop our dormant talents and provides energy to be on the path of growth and evolution.

The worldly ways have attuned the mind to think that the physical presence of another is required to ward off loneliness and if it is not there then fear takes over. Loneliness should not be taken as something negative, rather it is an opportunity to discover, your true self. One can create a connection with the aura of an evolved person by thinking or reading about them. On doing this, one can be propelled towards newness. The link with an evolved person who may be is a master of music, an artist or a successful entrepreneur can impart inspiration and enhance the spirit.

The one who is on the path of inner growth will always welcome time alone.

At a time in life I too completely withdrew. The external world seemed full of noise and beyond my comprehension – the simple beauty, clarity of life and love for others seemed to have been overcome with hypocrisy, resentment and unnecessary pretence. Then my sadhna to make sense of the world began.

As I lay in drowned in tears, praying for the way forward, a voice deep within directed me to get up and start writing. Soon it became and obsession, I wrote everything from the mundane to the profound. Clarity started to dawn and messages became evident. The most intense realisation was that if one is following the four unshakeable pillars of truth love karm - action and light then one can never feel lonely. These soon became the basis of everything in life.

The sadhna of truth and working on these four guidelines is the biggest strength and enormous source of energy. Truth, love karm and light are the gates to enter new realms of revelation and realisation. To me, it became amply clear that Param Bodhi, the Supreme Intellect never bestows anything on us that is frivolous. Loneliness is a steppingstone towards absolute tranquillity that leads to deeper realisation and enlightenment.

৪৩

Chapter 3

OUR WORLD IS A CREATION OF OUR THOUGHTS

Amit was an aspiring yogacharya. He worked hard and created a beautiful ashram that had the potential to become a refuge for those seeking calm and rejuvenation. The place had been donated to him by someone. But one fine day his greatest fear became true, his ashram was taken over by the one who claimed to be the real owner of the land. Faith and circumstances went against Amit and he was shocked at the turn of events. Although he was spiritually a strong person, he could not handle his emotions and went into depression. His spirit broke and he withdrew from the world.

There are many times in life when we experience our fears becoming our reality. So it is essential to be conscious of our thinking pattern as this can create a path for growth or denouement. Observe thoughts, analyse opinions and ideas truthfully and be centred in them, because they have the power to attract similar information and to resurrect themselves. Preconceived notions can attract messages and situations to firm up our views, thus it is important to stay open till we are not fully aware of the Truth. If one settles for incomplete knowledge or preconceived notions or reads between the lines, then such thoughts and ideas alone will continued to be nourished. This is how demonic thoughts are born and are perpetuated, just like the admirers of a successful or a famous person will find more and more reasons to become his ardent followers and detractors will find various reasons to be critical of him. Know that this has nothing to do with the karma of the celebrity; it is the seed of the thought within, which is ripening, hence, things happen to validate that prefixed view. It is a trap in which people get stuck as the circle of similar thoughts finds assurance by the mind thus repeatedly leaving no scope for liberation, openness and expansion.

Our world is the creation of our thoughts. No one can mould our world from outside. No moment should pass when we are not eliminating something from within, taking something to perfection, and creating something anew, because Nature is constantly doing the same. To be in sync with Nature, we must do this sadhana of creation, perfection and destruction. So, it is up to us whether to stagnate or create a better roadmap for growth.

Have faith in your sankalps, resolutions; dridh nishchay, being firm; and follow the 'one point programme' i.e. have absolute clarity about your goals so you can do justice to human life. And after establishing the sankalp, resolution, there is no need to doubt or question happenings. If the connection is strong and consistent, then Param Bodhi, the Supreme Intelligence, will arrange everything which helps to fulfil that resolve. It may be a test or a message to reassure the path. Be in dhyan to derive messages and directives out of it. With absolute surrender, dhyan will impart clarity and guidance. For this kind of sadhna, consistent practice is required which is different from tapasya, which is penance.

Tapasya is hectic, done along with severe austerity for a certain period. It is observed for a goal, to achieve an aim, fulfil a desire, get a boon, or acquire some siddhi, accomplishment. Sadhna is something that must be done lifelong for refinement that leads to full blossoming of human potential. It is a constant, perpetual, never-ending process, growing along with time and tide, like the mechanism of the Universe and laws of Nature, towards transformation and evolution.

༺༻

Chapter 4

WHY GET AFFECTED BY OTHERS?

Naina was constantly looking for the approval of others. Despite being in a good job and settled in all aspects, she would ask the opinion of others in everything she embarked upon. Decision making became a problem and soon she found herself totally confused and in duality. She seemed to have forgotten that she was blessed with capabilities to find and chalk her own path.

In spirituality, sensitivity increases as we evolve, but it does not mean we should get affected by what others say or do. Coming out of every situation is a learning. Everyone is caught in their own chakravyu – maze of thoughts and actions. The responsibility of the increase or decrease of its hold vests in our own thought process that constantly appears to access actions, reactions and situations as per our tuning and evolution. There is nothing right or wrong, everything is relative.

Then there are those who analyse situations in detail. For them, every problem has a very logical and precise solution. They think of all the pros and cons, and then the pros and cons of these pros and cons …. the cycle seems endless!

Getting more philosophical, with no proactive action to follow up the realisations, lead to being lost and confused. This implies that the seed of our thoughts is incorrect and frivolous, as it creates more rumination, doesn't convey any pleasantness, tries only to be convincing, instigating more mental dialogue. Only pleasant thoughts create pleasantness.

If in our conduct there is no effortlessness, it needs to be reviewed. Overthinking creates chaos and lack of clarity, leading to doubts. Duality kills spontaneity.

Loneliness is often a result of isolating oneself from the world due to overthinking, judging others and even being critical of one's own actions. This leads to misunderstandings and strained relationships. It is better to be clear of our own needs and desires. Problems arise when we want others to behave and perform as per our expectations. Generally people feel ignored and unwanted because they want others to be at their beck and call. When this does not happen frustration and loneliness sets in. We cannot make others happy, just like others' are not responsible for our happiness. A simple example is of air travel, one of the lifesaving rules that is emphasised is, wear your oxygen mask first before helping others even an infant is not an exception.

ॐ

Chapter 5

CLARITY AND PURITY

Clarity and Purity

Open

The Gates of Light

Charm and beauty of Truth Conquer

The darkness and ignorance Strangling the world

True light always flashes

and takes everyone by surprise

Defeating the calculations of Human Minds

Change is Inevitable

Events are happenings

At very subtle level

Slow and steady but for sure

To shower blessings on those TRUTHFUL and PURE

To create a future full

Of Love and Light

By dispelling the darkness

Destroying the imperfections

And to make Falsehoods see rejection

The Time Wheel of Nature Is ready

For amputation

To clear the path

For true assertions

This is the TRUTH

౩ఌ

Chapter 6

EGO IS NEEDY BUT SOUL IS NOT

The greatest cause of pain, strife and loneliness is ego. Pride can be both positive and negative and ego is a negative form of pride. This ego is knowing and believing what you are not. When inertia, hurt, anger, depression, pain, violence dominates us then we are not in the right state of being. Another self comes in-between our true self and divinity; that is ego. Ego is a weakness; it limits growth and creates stagnancy. It seeks constant approval from others and is energy consuming in its maintenance. The desire to control, possess, resent or use disagreements to trigger off personal imagination or opinions never reflects pious love. It gives rise to attachment. In attachment, needs cover the soul. It creates layers of ignorance which hampers growth and blossoming into our true self. We have trouble letting go of things and happenings due to the ego of 'doer-ship,' little realising that separation or detachment is not something to be feared. It is a test of time given to us to realise how strongly we are connected to our true self. The state of being away from our soul surfaces in separation, and the pain experienced is attachment. So, it is also a form of fear.

The soul is above fear and attachment. It has an eternal quality of spreading truth, love and light for which it requires no external support. If we are out of 'doer-ship' which is a habit of always taking credit – 'I did this, I did that' and ego, then we are centered in our true self and no fear can affect us. When we stop analysing others, whether they live up to our expectations or not, resist controlling situations, correcting the mistakes of others and advising and instructing others. This is the first step towards realising the gunas - attributes of one's soul.

The person who lives in the attributes of the soul, gives, gives and gives just like Nature, without asking for anything in return. Spreading joy unconditionally, not seeking the approval of others, such a person lives for a higher cause, driven by a sacred love that does not aspire for selfish gains. This is a state of supreme non-attachment. So, leave the desire to control and aspire for freedom. Resentment arises with a need to control, letting free or letting go is love.

ೞಀಊ

Chapter 7

WHY SPOIL YOUR
FACE FOR OTHERS' FOLLIES?

If a thought is creating tension, it should be dropped. Someone is being toxic, step away. We have the choice to do this and be comfortable, peaceful, tranquil and undisturbed in any situation. Why create ripples all the time and then suffer the consequences of tension, pain, resentment, anger and fear? Why spoil our health and personality in the bargain? Instead of taking sleeping pills or anxiety medication that give temporary relief, one needs to find a mental state experiencing peace and tranquillity.

When one is sincerely working on the self, then the key for equanimity in being in surrender to the moment. Think: 'yeh aisa hi hona hoga' – this is the way it was meant to be.

Learning is joy. Every situation has come to teach us something, look for the message it is imparting. Our thought process should be such: 'Prabhu, auron ko sheetal karein, aapou sheetal hoi' – O Supreme, may I bring peace to others and be at peace with myself.

We don't allow life to happen and bring mind created arguments or ideas and assumptions into everything, which is why we face so many ups and downs. Observe everything like a witness.

Sukh, happiness, dukh, sadness are all part of our thought process. There are so many benevolent things, so many good things, waiting to seep in to make us peaceful, tranquil, joyful. If it is not happening, it means only one thing – we have not been able to empty ourselves of our past. Our subconscious has to be emptied. The state of being empty and light, has not been experienced.

Life is a beautiful journey that consists of ups and downs. Each event is symbolic. It carries a message, a meaning that is divine in itself, that no worldly words can define. Only realised people know this, that is why there is a permanent smile on their faces, as if stating 'O human you cry and pity yourself, but you have no idea what I went through to earn this smile.'

৪০৫৪

Chapter 8

EVERYTHING IS PERFECT!

Nothing is frivolous. Every moment is joy. Know that it has come to create bliss, or to teach something. 'Mast raho harr situation mein' – be joyous and comfortable in every situation.

Although the moment was not chosen by us, we can still choose what to do with it. Whatever is coming forth, it should be pleasant. Even in Shri Krishn's life there were moments when people were nasty, rude and downright insulting. But he stayed calm, without losing his equipoise. From that vantage point of peace and equanimity, he could see the larger picture and it gave him the ability to select the most viable course of action.

So, even in a situation that is very taxing, always think of 'How to make others comfortable' – just thinking this will reduce irritability. The focus should not be on an individual but making the whole situation pleasant and amiable. Getting affected by a situation creates ripples.

The guru mantra is always:

Being saral, sahaj, samanya, sadharan, swabhavik and sanyamit. True spirituality culminates through these six attributes of a human:

1. Saral (being simple): Complications come when we slide into acquired behaviour and act to maintain a certain image either to 'fit in' or to satisfy the ego.

2. Sahaj (spontaneous): An innate attribute to sail through every situation with ease, peace and grace. The opposite of sahaj is asahaj (being in discomfort). This saps energy. Sahajta, innate spontaneity comes when we have been working on ourselves. Our conduct and reach of our aura should bring others into the flow also so they can look at life through a positive lens.

3. Samanya (normal in every state, staying equipoised in all situations, positive or negative).

4. Sadharan (being ordinary as all other beings): 'I am as others, not any one special'. Problems come when we try to appear special by going into doer-ship or by fanning our ego and, in the process, show others down, as if they are lesser beings.

5. Swabhavik: This is an intrinsic attribute, to behave according to one's natural nature, 'I am natural, and I behave like nature', giving joy to all.

6. Sanyamit – To be disciplined and have a regular routine.

Children set a perfect example for these attributes. They are simple, spontaneous, uncomplicated, forgiving, truthful and trusting. Even if a person approaches a baby with a knife, the baby will continue to smile and play, even try to playfully grab the weapon thinking it to be a toy. These are laws of nature and get tested when we conduct ourselves in this world. If we don't become – saral, sahaj, swabhavik, sadharan, samanya and sanyamit – any amount of spiritual knowledge will not help us evolve.

Judge for yourself! Fewer the ripples, the less affected one is. Spread joy, only then will there be bliss because we are all connected with each other. There are certain things in life that cost nothing – love, forgiveness, joy, concern, compassion and consideration. When we work to spread these, there cannot be any loneliness. The world becomes one big family and everything – matter and being become mediums of the divine, assisting and propelling us ahead for newness in our worldly journey.

Na kahu sey dosti, na kahu sey bair – no friendly ties with anyone, nor having animosity towards anyone.

How we conduct ourselves that will invoke supreme grace, should be our concern. When we have not been effortless, the times when we have considered ourselves superior to others and different from them – all these instances are the cause of our strife and creating karmic bondages.

Loneliness comes when we invite undue complications and doubt everything. It is we who complicate the simplicity of life and make it heavy and overbearing.

ॐ

Chapter 9

OUR LIFE IS PERFECTLY DESIGNED FOR GROWTH

Nature never gives what we desire and want, but it surely gives us what we need and is necessary for our growth.

Let me share an episode about the birth of butterfly and the profound wisdom it entails.

A man saw a butterfly's cocoon, which was almost mature. In a while he observed a small opening in it, the time for the butterfly to appear from the chrysalis had arrived. To experience this unique phenomenon of Nature and to observe the butterfly take its first flight, he sat there in amazement.

For hours the butterfly tried emerging from that small opening and kept withdrawing inside. The man could not take its prolonged arduous strife anymore, and out of compassion he slit the cocoon. The butterfly hopped out easily, but its body was swollen, full of fluid and its wings were small and shriveled up.

He kept watching, would it fly, would it fly now? He wanted to experience the joy of seeing its first flight.

But nothing like that happened. The butterfly kept rolling and stumbling all its life. The man then realised Nature's law and the science behind it. His eagerness in showing his benevolence by being a doer had resulted in the butterfly's life becoming an unfortunate curse. The natural effort of trying to come out of the little opening was essential for the butterfly. The effort ensured that the internal fluids in its body were squeezed and transferred to the wings providing them with necessary moisture and volume which would assist in opening the wings and subsequently lifting the weight of its body. The result of interfering in the working of Nature in the name of compassion can be cruel and painful. This is the truth of all efforts that are against Nature.

Know that the life we have has been blessed with, the Supreme Organiser, Supreme Designer or Supreme Arranger.

We are meant to evolve, know ourselves, work on our growth through this given life alone. Nothing can be removed from it or changed as per our wishes. What we have to do is to use it the best way possible. Do not think about what is missing because when we keep working on ourselves (which is what the Supreme wants to us to do), we will be guided to our quest. So be in surrender.

We need very little to survive, rest is all lust. Whatever we have, has been bestowed with how best to use it, that is what we need to keep in mind. If the Supreme has given only as much as is barely enough for one person, it means time has not yet come to share it. The main thing is to work on the self, know ourselves, know our likes, dislikes, strengths and weaknesses. Our path of growth lies through that alone. As we become more and more deserving, we keep getting opportunities for further growth in that field. Main thing is to be deserving. To develop our sensitivities, cut out the frills, needless show of anger, wasting time, that stops us from becoming a pure human. We have to do this sadhna-consistent practice. We must become pure humans. The Supreme will take care of the rest.

Our free will lies only in our choice, either we use our mind and avoid the situations we are meant to go through; or go through them to the best of our ability, learn from them and grow. That is the only selection we need to make.

Take the example of a tree. It does not have a choice. The seed once sown grows in the soil it has been planted in; it takes water and nutrition from that soil alone, the rest is taken care by Nature. Humans must only be in gratitude that they have been given this life to become Bhagwat Swaroop - like divinity, so as to blossom fully. The more we flourish the closer we will get to the divine qualities, and the catch is that the closer we get, 'Supreme will' becomes 'thy will', and 'thy will' becomes 'Supreme will'. This is beautiful natural mechanism.

Many times people want to meet me, while I am in deep dhyan. Being in surrender, I take it as a divine call and allow them to visit. But because of my intense truthful aspiration to be on my own, somehow, the other person will call and cancel due to some reason or the other. This is how this system works. We only need to become deserving of the divine grace. I want everyone to experience this state of effortlessness and gratitude. When the divine is there to hear our call, why worry and feel lonely!

८०८३

THY WILL

My will is thy will

Thy will is my will

Thy work is my work

My work is thy work

My love is thy love

Thy love is my love

Thy truth is my truth

My truth is thy truth

I am thy

Thy am I

THE EYE

THY

KNOW YOUR QUEST

First it is important to know the quest. What are you searching for? Know your truth. Have faith that Supreme will provide us with everything to realise that truth. We have to traverse through the problems we come across on the course to reach the truth that we are seeking like a treasure hunt. Every situation is perfectly designed and sent to enhance the path of evolution.

When we go through whatever comes in front of us to the best of our ability, in perfect surrender, clarity dawns. We are not here to negate any situation but to sail through it with ease, peace, and grace.

The thought that through puja, or some rituals things will become easier, is fine for those whose search is limited to finding just sukh, happiness or simply ensuring that their house, business and family, everything runs smoothly. But for those who have a different quest, are seeking more about the truth of life and existence, they will have to realise that all situations and tests are mediums to propel us towards higher truths. Whatever gyan we get, we need to live it, realise it, and move on. Negate, doubt or question nothing.

Some people try to prevent situations from manifesting or try to circumvent them through tantrik rituals, while others, on the path of evolution use the same rituals, mantras, sound vibrations and yantras, empowered configurations, to experience the situations fully and realise the truth. The great avatars, Shri. Ram and Shri. Krishn were powerful enough to change the course of their lives. But they chose the tougher route, lived like normal human beings, went through the trials and tribulations of life to become examples of idealistic, mature and unique handling of the challenges that life threw their way. Their purpose was to reinstate the laws of truth love karm and light in humanity.

One needs a lot of energy to go through life events – shakti, physical energy; will power; one point programme; gyan, wisdom; ananya bhakti, unflinching devotion; and faith; a faith that does not waiver, is able to see the subtle, subtler and subtlest messages for growth and evolution that life events convey.

Shri Krishn used his time alone, while tending to his cows to master the flute, play and bond with his peers and even clean up the river, ridding it of a dreaded snake. Shri Ram, while in exile did sadhna to protect the innocent rishis and other righteous habitants of the forest and to increase his arsenal of weapons, empowering himself for the impending war with Ravan.

These are examples of humans who accepted their fate with a smile and continue to evolve by living each challenge that life threw at them to the best of their mental and physical capacities. If they had succumbed to being lonely, wallowed in self-pity, negating all karm they would surely not accomplish their divine destiny – purposeful life.

Problems are tests of one's strength to endeavour and while navigating challenges, one acquires the capacity to overcome them and grow. To deny this natural process an opportunity to blossom and bear fruit only encourages karamheenta or indolence.

We ask the Supreme for strength, he gives us difficulties to make us capable and courageous; we ask for wisdom and sadbuddhi or good senses to prevail, he gives us problems to unravel; we ask for samruddhi, prosperity, he has given us a mind and an aptitude for work; we ask for love he gives us all his people to spread warmth; we ask the Supreme for boons, he gives us umpteen chances to make them happen.

In mythological stories when God appears, gives *darshan*, he asks the devotee what boon he would like. O foolish human! Doesn't God know what you desire? That Omniscient One wants you to ask for a boon just to know what your mind is capable of asking! In your want is hidden you supatrata, your worthiness. Herein lies the secret of the constitution of our destiny. So do not become a beggar, become warriors of deeds, no effort is beyond our capacities. This is the truth of our satta, our existence.

The purpose of life is in front of us, what Prabhu has given us, is the path that will unveil the true purpose of our life, we must accept it. Everything comes out of the moment, not by negating it but by going through it, clarity dawns. So, we only have to only accomplish the moment. Many such moments chalk out the course of our lives.

For this, stay unaffected from situations, be aware and witness them, seek shakti, energy; gyan, knowledge by being in bhakti – devotion, connected and in absolute surrender.

Each person must find their own calling, and this is what makes one unique. We all are alone in our quest, but never intended to be lonely!

Chapter 12

ATTACHMENT AND DETACHMENT

It is important to first understand the reason for attachment only then we can move towards detachment.

We go through life forming various relationships…some near and dear. These trigger expectations creating a set pattern of behaviours, like a mother is expected to behave in a certain way or a child is expected to have a set pattern of conduct… Thus everyone falls in a certain category of expectations from each other. When this does not happen we feel let down, burdened, sad, stuck and starts holding others accountable for not meeting the set standards of that relationship, creating anger, blame and negativity. We are quick to put each other in a witness box and pass judgements about the behaviour and expectations without first looking at our own selves first.

Attachments are self-created. Let me share a story of 'The Frog and Little Pond.' The frog living in a tiny pond was always feeling stuck with his family and few other frogs around him.

Then one day he took a great leap and pushed himself out of the pond landing into a lake. Here he met other frogs, variety of fish and other creatures, he experienced new sights and sounds and felt an expansion within his being. He learnt new skills to adapt to the lake and in doing so he felt a sense of growth and joy. At times, he would become sad thinking of his companions in the little pond but he his sense of newness and mental expansion always overpowered his negative emotions. He was still very attached to his family and companions of the small pond but this attachment did not feel like a burden as it earlier would. When he went back for a visit to meet them, his inner joy touched everyone around him and the frog felt a sense of detachment through his attachment.

When there is "to and fro" in our little ponds we create expectations attachments limitations and restraints for ourselves and others. Then each individual falls in a set category and has to stand up to the measure of performance within that relationship.

Do not invite depression by thinking about attachment and detachment instead work to change and evolve. Perform duty karm sincerely but without creating stress for ourselves because when we over do things or go out of the way to do something for others, we also increase our bar of expectations and when this is not met, we feel let down and hold others responsible for our shortcomings and pain.

Emotions turn to attachments when we stay limited to mine and thine within our little ponds. For example why just pray for your own child? Expand your prayers and pray for all the children around you. This simple expansion of thought will reduce attachment with one particular individual and connect you to the entire world! The whole world becomes a family.

Nature has given us emotions not to negate or renounce, but to refine, evolve and flourish through them. If these emotions or rasas were unessential, then Nature in its evolutionary process would have eliminated them. Emotions are gifts of nature and are not to be renounced but to be channelised for our betterment and to help serve others.

Attract joy to yourself by spreading joy to others. Don't limit yourself but expand your aura and flow like the river where water never stagnates. Make emotions your strength and give them a new direction for growth glory and grace.

When we are detached from our little pools and attached to the whole world in equal measure, then everything, matter and being become a part of our larger family. This was how it was in Bharat till a few decades ago. One person's grandmother was the grandmother of the entire locality. Therefore, the trials and tribulations of one family became the matter of concern for everyone and they all stepped in to help. When there is such concern, compassion and consideration, who can be lonely!

Chapter 13

BE DETACHED

Disconnecting from things which affect us to stay unaffected is the first step. This is not indifference; it is an informed choice to empower oneself to go through a demanding situation. The next step is to remain unmoved because it is possible that the person or the situation will continue to drain our energy.

True spirituality ordains that we stay unaffected, witness everything and be aware that the situation exists and will take the time to pass. Through ananya bhakti – unflinching devotion that is unique, as it is different for everyone, the Supreme will provide the gyan, knowledge and wisdom of how to sail through. 'It is there, this is truth, but I will stay unaffected, Prabhu has given me shakti – power, the shakti is in me, it exists, and I am aware of it,' should be the prayer.

We need shakti and gyan and for this, prayer is needed. Be in gratitude of the situation, for it has come to propel us towards the next experience for growth. Then, being aware and witnessing things unfolding, the need for gyan to go through the situation becomes evident. Gyan can dawn only through bhakti – a deep communion with the Supreme. True gyan cannot be acquired, it descends when dhyan and bhakti merge.

The Supreme imparts messages through some clues. I have experienced that whenever a question or a situation arose in life, some magazine, book or information on how to go through the problem would reach me and clarity would dawn. When we work on ourselves in all sincerity, everything around becomes a guru, and life becomes interesting. There is no time for laziness, boredom or loneliness. Life is a university, supreme is the invigilator and we are the students...

So far people have studied various scriptures, and there is no dearth of knowledge, but now it is time to narrow down to the gist of this moment. While leading life, one needs information and knowledge to deal with situations. There is no need to memorise all the scriptures, just live in the moment. One is not here to accomplish anything or go anywhere. All fears and insecurities are the result of living in the mind and not in the moment. We all will die one day and at the end, what will matter is our last thought before passing, which will be according to the life one has led and will sow the seed for next sojourn of life on Earth. So, it is important to live each given moment to perfection.

ॐ

Chapter 14

THE FEELING OF HOLLOWNESS

Despite being surround by a lot of information, luxuries and latest gadgets, humans are experiencing a strange kind of emptiness, stagnancy in their inner self because the time wheel has turned; it is moving towards a new age of genuineness, truth, love and light.

Intelligent people are feeling this more because they have been living by using the mind, logic and artificial ways of life that have driven them away from Nature. They are unhappy even after acquiring so many inventions, knowledge, wealth and material comforts. All this is because spiritual growth has stagnated, there is a disconnect between the soul and the conscious self of the being. Humanity is disconnected from Mother Nature and a natural way of life. Depression and other mental illnesses are on the rise because we have forgotten to relate to the main and the biggest source of energy – Nature. When we do not work to live in the attributes of the soul – unconditional love, truth and light then it is normal to feel hollow, restless, seeking something outside… hoping to find answers that lead to fulfillment.

When depression and hollowness set in, we fail to imbibe the qualities of Mother Nature and to connect with the soul which is constantly seeking growth, evolution and liberation. Then seeking to release itself from the unproductive body, the soul attracts unexpected diseases or mishaps.

Depression and other mental and physical ailments should be taken as warnings from the soul that one needs to go inwards. A productive life – doing justice to human birth is a life of spirituality and not religiosity. Spirituality and laws of Nature are truth, love, karm and light.

Satya – Truth, taken from Satyug, the Golden Age of purity: Embodies the purity and innocence of the Golden Age, where truth and authenticity reign supreme.

Being truthful means having perfect synchronicity between thoughts words and deeds. At any given time, all three need to be aligned, so that what is being thought, the same is spoken, followed by the related action. There is no ambiguity and undercurrents in expression. Everything is stated in clear, humble and kind words that are full of love. So, the focus is to state the truth that has been imbibed, lived and experienced. Be a living example of this.

Prem – Love is taken from Tretayug. This encourages us to cultivating the love and compassion that characterised the Silver Age, where relationships and harmony flourished.

Love is unconditional. Pure love is spontaneous, simple, effortless and without any fear of mental, social or moral bondage, desire, need and expectation. It entails loving and respecting matter and being. Be a constant giver like Nature, offering without any calculations. Seeing and feeling with gratitude, the Supremes' design, grace and glory everywhere. This highest form of love is guided by true wisdom and bestows bliss and joy.

Karm–Action from Dwaparyug, ordains embracing the principle of righteous action and duty that defined the Copper Age, where human beings learnt to balance individual and collective responsibilities.

It means living each moment to perfection, utilsing all our mental and physical capacities to the maximum – joyfully as an offering to Supreme.

Prakash–Light from Kaliyug, stands for illuminating the path with the light of knowledge, awareness, and spiritual growth that was accelerated in the Iron Age, where humanity was challenged to evolve and transcend.

It also stands for removal of all ignorance, hypocrisy, falsehood, pre-conceived notions, guilt and fear to become weightless, so as to get filled with Supreme Light. Light is not indulging in things that hinder our growth and are not for the welfare of all, do not lead to clarity and liberation. It is a direct connection with that Supreme energy which is an unending divine source of energy and a giver of all life forms. When connected, it propels one to eradicate all artificial behaviour, hypocrisy and age-old mind tunings. It encourages us to 'be light'.

These four principles, which I collectively call as Mana Marg offers a holistic and evolutionary approach to spiritual growth, allowing individuals to navigate the complexities of modern life while staying grounded in timeless wisdom, to be connected to true inner self and Supreme Consciousness and to be deserving mediums of natural process of growth transformation and evolution.

Let us aspire to sail through every situation with ease, peace, and grace on our journey of life, allowing us to grow and evolve into our highest potential.

Human beings have to change according to Nature's designs and be absolutely open to it. In the present age we have become so accustomed to being dismantled into separate parts, just like doctors who treat only a specific part of the human body in which they specialise in, not considering the human body as a whole! Similarly, our ego and 'doer-ship,' divide us and we feel superior-inferior, big-small, higher-lower and generally not a part of a larger whole.

Humanity in the present scenario has to change according to Nature's design as the Time wheel is turning. Be open to Nature's laws otherwise we will not know what to do and who to turn to resolve the inner hollowness and conflict between the inner and the outer spaces. It is this separation from our source that creates suffering, conflict, lack of purpose and emptiness in life.

The knock of hollowness or something amiss should be taken as a positive indication that one is being nudged towards change and we need to introspect, course correct and reconnect to our ancient values and ways of spirituality according to Nature's design.

𝕭𝕮

Chapter 15

SUFFERING

Those who take the shelter of being lonely often talk about sorrow and suffering and look to blame others for their misery gaining sympathy by portraying themselves as victims in their lives, but never try to explore the cause behind this.

Let us try to find out what is sorrow? There is no mention of the word suffering in our Vedic Scriptures. Difficulties of life did not give rise to sorrow, instead were accepted gracefully as the Divine will. Nature is very benevolent. She sends forth situations that help us evolve and cut our accumulated karmas. So why negate the difficulties in life?

This word 'suffering' became popular around the time of Mahatma Buddh, when people began to assume that hardships, that were being experienced were suffering, something that was forced upon their lives by external forces. This belief then made life tough as the true reason for their presence was overlooked. Our being attracts these events to help us cut our accumulated karma and when done with ease peace and grace, these propel us towards the next level of evolution. This process is so important that even rishis-munis, when they wanted to achieve some realisation, would leave their ashrams and sit in the caves doing tapasya to gain true knowledge, seek enlightenment, become brahm gyanis or the Enlightened Ones for example.

This penance is for the purification of the body, mind and soul. Know the truth by abstaining the body and mind of sensual gratification.

Chapter 16

REPENTANCE, ATONEMENT AND GRATITUDE FOR REFINEMENT OF LIFE

In our everyday lives, the words 'sorry and thank you' are often used mechanically, stripped of the deep emotions they are meant to convey. These words, while part of common etiquette, have become overused and superficial, reducing their significance to mere niceties. Without genuine intent, they fail to fulfil their true purpose of emotional connection and self-awareness.

Saying sorry is meant to express regret for causing harm or inconvenience and to atone for one's wrongdoings. It signifies realisation, repentance, and a commitment to self-improvement. However, the casual use of sorry diminishes its power, making it a 'lightweight' word that neither fosters introspection nor motivates change.

Ancient Hindu texts offer deeper practices of repentance, known as pashchatap, repentance and prayaschitt, atonement. These practices are not merely verbal expressions of regret; they involve introspection and actions to rectify mistakes. The word sorry when used lightly or causally does not create any room for self-improvement or introspection. But pashchatap and then prayashchitt send a mental message to the victim also that the wrong doer has owned up and is repenting for atonement. This creates an environment of forgive and forget.

Procedure for Pashchatap—The feeling of repentance requires continuity in our thought process. Keeping in mind where the mistake was committed or where the behaviour was inappropriate, or contrary to the natural nature and in accordance with rules of proper conduct.

The first thing which happens when we realise that we have done something wrong is to feel guilty, which is natural. The feeling of guilt, fear and anxiety can stunt out spiritual growth. One should transform guilty into gratitude for the opportunity to refine our attributes. It is also time bestowed by nature to reconnect with our true Vedic heritage, read our scriptures perform rituals like havans etc, that are an outcome of the eternal Vedic culture. These assist us to be centred, to see the light, look within…work on the body mind soul, sowing the seed of service and gratitude.

Pashchatap is a form of spiritual detox. It is a full psychological treatment for oneself. To throw out the body's toxins and to eliminate dependency on certain things which may be retarding our growth. For example, we are dependent on tea or coffee to kick start our day or need a certain atmosphere or colleagues to accomplish our work.

The main goal of pashchatap is purification, however, if done in the right manner it teaches detachment, non-indulgence, and even helps us to tune our system to positivity and purity which brings clarity. Pashchatap is a way to empty our subconscious mind. It is something we have to levy on ourselves. Earlier gurus would ask the disciples who were at fault, what method and means would they choose for pashchatap and prayashchit to repent for their mistakes. It could also be sewa, service of the guru or the community, or retreat into silence and dhyan, or isolate, or give up some food or pleasure.

Procedure for Prayashchit–Steps adopted to atone for the mistakes in order to free the subconscious of every spec and burden of guilt. It can be done at three levels of the body, mind and the soul.

At the physical level, it can be done by identifying something that one cannot do without and give it up. For example, one can give up a favourite food item, certain dresses, bodily comforts or certain behaviours, like going into silence for the chosen period of time. The duration can be anything from three days to forty days. For grave matters, pashchatap can be done till one feels light and relived.

At the mind level, during this time it is important to engage in the study of shastras, for example, the Geeta, Ramayan and the Vedas and do chintan mannan or contemplate on them. Rituals like havan can also be done, but without entertaining any feeling of guilt or fear.

At the soul level, for atma shuddhi, to cleanse the inner self, nirantar jap – continuous mantra chanting also helps. It is important to remember not to think about the wrong that has been committed to someone and feel guilty about it, instead, think that Prabhu has bestowed an opportunity to purify your being and be grateful for it.

By doing prayashchit in the right way we feel a sense of oneness with others and realise the universality of thoughts. Knowing that we are as much capable of making mistakes as anyone else, it cuts down the ego, stops us from judging others harshly, creating a sense of oneness with others.

THE LIMITATIONS OF THANK YOU

The other most frequently used word is thank you. Thank you is a way to acknowledge and appreciate the actions of others. However, it is often used out of habit or, worse, it can be used as a form of sarcasm. In contrast, the concept of Aabhar, gratitude, in Hindu philosophy elevates gratitude to a deeper, spiritual level.

Aabhar, gratitude is an expression of heartfelt acknowledgement, humility, and appreciation for the blessings received. Unlike *thank you*, which can sometimes inflate ego, Aabhar fosters humility and reduces the sense of doer-ship. True gratitude teaches one to look at the positives in life and allows one to be above the negative aspects. Gratitude unknowingly increases the power of acceptance of all life happenings without being affected. Such feelings encourage surrender to the Divine ways. And as the popular saying goes "Man ka ho to achha, aur agar Uske man ka ho to aur bhi achha." Translated as, if things happen according to your wishes that is good, but if they happen according to the Divine wishes then it is the best. So be in gratitude for everyone who imparts an opportunity to improve and enhance life.

To find the inner strength and the will to improve one needs sadhna (regular practice to master something with continuity and perseverance). It is not time-bound. It is related to concentration and is applied to perfect something, like one masters a yog asan, learning music or even writing.

To conclude, pashchatap, prayashchit and sadhna are all activites that are done in 'me time'. It is therefore important to ensure that time alone is used productively to help us come out of our various guilts and fears. Simply rejecting the gift of time alone as an imposition and an unfortunate happening reflects a lazy, stagnant attitude.

Leisure time or 'me time' is the time for progress. Our evolution depends on how we spend our spare time. Aspire to make leisure time the most creative moments. Time for karm - action is like worship time. If done honestly with concentration using all mental and physical capacities to the maximum, it is the highest offerings to the Supreme.

Just be yourself, true self!

Be your own friend

Cherish your own company

Enjoy your leisure to the maximum.

Embrace loneliness and use it wisely to grow and glow!

౭౦౧౮

Chapter 17

PRAYER FOR SERENITY

May I see the sunshine

When the storm seems unending

May I feel serenity and tranquillity

In this world so difficult to understand

May I get strength to walk through life

By the pain and conflict

I experience

May I face new situations with

Courage and optimism

May I discover enough goodness in Others

In creating world of peace

May I offer a kind word

A reassuring touch

And a sweet smile

As a gift to all

May I have the courage and wisdom

To follow the teachings of

All evolved souls

May I learn from each encounter

With others

Long and short

May I be able to see the beauty all around

May I feel the lacking in present

Become fulfilling in future

May I always sense the feel of

Belonging to the

Supreme Lord

This is the truth of my being

Live dangerously to be alive

Live joyously to be alive

Live without fear to be alive

Live without guilt to be alive

Just be alive

ALIVE

✿

Chapter 18

EMOTIONS ARE ENERGY

Every emotion, every thought is like a ripple in calm or placid water of consciousness. From each thought idea emotion one can ignite the fire within, rejuvenate our own system.

But there is a general misconception that if someone cries or shouts, he is doing so to demand something. When a child cries, we think he needs something, food, milk, we don't see that as a natural cry – to let him cry a bit so that he moves his arms and legs, do some sort of activity; since he has been fed and changed on time. A mother knows that we need not link every cry with a demand, otherwise children start believing that if they want attention, they must cry. She knows that it could be a cry or restlessness for a new exercise, may be to turn themselves in bed. When an animal's baby is born, it gets up on its feet very quickly, but human babies lay on their back for several months before they can sit, crawl and stand on their feet.

Do not always link the cry of a baby with physical or mental need, link it to some inner spiritual need. Perhaps it is a cry for growth. It is the same for adults. Our mind may not know this, but the answer lies in creativity. It is very important for everyone to be creative. Just like the Universe has convulsions and something nice and new is created, similarly, the cry of restlessness in a human could mean reflection for spiritual evolution, growth. Hellen Keller was visually impaired, hearing impaired, yet she managed to accomplish a lot. Her example reassures us that the divine always opens other doors if one is closed. We only have to be centred, open and ponder over it.

When we make others happy, we become happy; it is a lovely cycle.

If we don't get happiness and consequently stop giving happiness to others – we will never be happy. It indicates that what we have not got, if we start giving that to others, it will come back to us! The bhav-thought behind it should be truthful and full of love. If we are large hearted and generous with others, then Nature will be generous with us. Our generosity and kindness will never go waste; it goes on circulating. So keep flowing, stagnancy proceeds to immobility.

Do sadhna of rising above the thought of 'mine and thine' and act without discrimination. This is real penance. It needs constant sadhna to not get affected by petty things. To stoop down to other people's level and react depletes our energy. That is why we feel low after some interactions. To maintain energy and cheerfulness always remain centred and unaffected by surroundings and undue happenings.

ॐ

Chapter 19

DEPRESSION: THE BASE CAMP FOR SELF-ANALYSIS

Science considers depression as an illness or disease, but spiritually, depression is a plateau given by Nature to know the true meaning and importance of detachment. In the complete life cycle of a human being, plateaus are sure to manifest at least seven to ten times, at an interval of eight to twelve years.

The four major phases of life i.e. Brahmacharya ashram, Grihastha ashram, Vanaprastha ashram and Sannyas ashram of our Vedic culture co-relate to this reality and mental state. This is a unique and miraculous law of Nature.

Four Ashrams are stages to get prepared for next stages in life for smooth sailing through the span of life and help individuals prepare for the next phase of their journey.

- The first is Brahmacharya - This comprises of learning exploring education, self-discipline, and spiritual growth by studying scriptures and great literature and realising the importance of Guru.

- The second is Grihastha - This entails fulfilling all duty karms, activities as householder or profession, the focus being on building a family, career, and contributing to society, making a mark in society.

- The third is Vanaprastha - It is similar to retirement from routine life, being completely peaceful, contended, nurturing the body, mind and spirit. It focuses on proper use of energy for enhancing and realising soul power for spiritual growth, introspection, and preparation for the next stage.

- The fourth and final stage, Sannyasa - It is that of living life as renunciate, focussing on complete dedication to spiritual pursuits, renouncing all attachments and indulgences. As a result of detaching with worldly relationships, a feeling of connection and merging with highest Entity, Supreme Truth becomes the core of existence.

These Ashrams serve as a framework for individuals to navigate the different stages of life, cultivating the necessary skills, wisdom, and spiritual growth for a fulfilling and purposeful life, justifying human form, a temple of Supreme divinity – Prabhu Tattve.

When each of these ashrams are not lived as ordained, there is imbalance in life and society as a whole, causing imbalances and creating hinderances in the smooth sailing of life.

In the state of depression, the human mind is disillusioned and astonished by worldly experiences. It is detached and is lost in its own world. The mind is either agitated and indulges in self-pity and may even think of suicide, or because of *aatma-manthan*, self-analysis, it could gather itself, and determined with new enthusiasm, give truthful direction towards a life of absolute awareness. It could even wander, seeking a true guru or mentor.

Western psychology has called the mental condition of staying away from the world in a state of inaction and indolence in the darkness of loneliness – as the disease of depression. This word is now used frequently in the common everyday language even by the young. Lost in the maze of tension, depression and boredom, they block all paths for growth.

For a truly spiritual person, this state of stagnation is not a disease. When a mentally evolved human finds the world meaningless, in other words, when the true face of the world becomes visible to an emotional and sensitive person, this state of plateau or 'camp' is created. Mental hurt is not the only reason for it. A break or hindrance in the mental, spiritual and economic growth can also be a reason for this condition.

A human who does some soul searching, meditation and contemplation rises from this plateau or base camp due to his own will power, soul power and gets a new lease of life, new energy. He moves forward towards growth and evolution, just like a mountaineer climbs to summit the highest peak.

Those who indulge and wallow in this state, get mentally unstable, and even can harm themselves. This is sin, an insult to the internal powers of human. It is difficult to know when depression is silently creeping into our lives. It starts by repeated feeling of virakti, indifference or boredom. The span of the intervals between the states of depression becomes less and less, and the dependency on medicines or outer means increases. When this happens, realise that the problem may have been suppressed but not fully resolved.

A wise person is the one who recognises these symptoms, does self-analysis, makes suitable changes in his routine and daily activities, maintains discipline and realising one's truth, is determined to never let growth stop, guided by the laws of Nature. This is true purusharth, endeavour. Life is a sadhna, penance, for this effort. Only the person who goes through depression and emerges as a better human being, can recognise and contribute towards humanity and can recognise and go through future plateaus, will take them as stepping stone for further growth.

Spiritually these plateaus are like base camps to release the unwanted baggage, to reach the topmost, highest peak. How can we ever reach the top of the peak, if we disintegrate on the way. Therefore, it is essential to learn to move forward with enthusiasm after complete rest and preparation at these base camps.

Jagaakar gyan yog, jalaakar vivek jyot

Naveenta se ho oat-proth barh ja suprabhat ki orr.

Ignite gyan yog, light the lamp of wisdom, and with renewed zeal, move ahead towards a new dawn.

ೞುೞ

Chapter 20

MECHANISM OF ENERGY

Sangeeta was constantly making plans. She was highly educated, young and enthusiastic but when it came to implementing her ideas, she was rarely left with any strength to follow them through. Sangeeta's friends thought her to be quixotic, because she lived in a dream world, making plans that never saw the light of day. Her days were spent talking about useless things, sometimes gossiping, eating out or visiting malls etc. She rarely seemed to be working towards her goals with a single-minded focus. Her family was worried about her.

We humans get pleasure when our mind wanders; daydreaming can be fun… and many times we don't even realise that it is happening. And we carry on… 'he said this', 'I will do this in turn'…and thoughts just keep spiralling in, never to leave. Swami Vivekananda said that the mind is like a restless monkey who has consumed hundreds of bottles of alcohol, and on top of that been stung by several scorpions…just imagine how it will behave. This is the state of a restless mind.

In the *Geeta*, Arjun says, the movement of the mind is very difficult to track, how can one manage the mind? To which Shri Krishna replies, sure it is difficult, I know, but this can be overcome with abhyas, practise. Give your mind the potion of '*Hari Naam.*' The moment it starts running around, grab it and ask it to chant *Hari Naam* or just pray.

Sometimes we exhaust ourselves thinking so much about an issue that we are left with no strength to do anything about it. The mind is very restless. Set it to task, so that it does not interfere with your dhyan and the brain is free to receive Universal Directives and have the strength to follow the teachings of evolved ones.

We might have the knowledge, means and the tools to perform tasks, but without shakti or energy we cannot accomplish anything. Everyone knows and understands that energy, strength and vitality are required for sustained physical or mental capacities. We all are living because of energy and we all deal with energy fluctuations of our bodies and mind on a daily basis. We are even surrounded by energy fields, from our phones, I-Pads to kitchen appliances, cars to space and the cosmos.

When we start walking the path of self-discovery it is very important to understand the mechanism of energy. Most of us know that we need to conserve our energy to continue functioning but usually end up spending this reservoir of power in mundane activities such as watching tv or shopping or gossiping etc. This is because we do not know what is the best way of spending it.

The optimal use of energy is for growth and expansion. Energy flows within us from a pure source. But we are mentally tuned to use it for selfish motives and mind designs/ mental schemes. There is no visible harm in this, however, it stops future growth and inner evolution because we become self-centred and create cobwebs of darkness around us limiting our creativity and expansion of truth, our real self. The precious energy we consume for mind games and ego boosts usually results in making us stagnant, anxious, stressful, fearful, diseased and depressed in the long run.

The Supreme mechanism is constantly working to provide pure energy to all. There is never any energy breakdown in its grid. Only we need to be tuned and open enough to be able to receive it. For this one must practice creating a void – absolute emptiness, where there are no thoughts, no ripples within. Practice doing this for 30 seconds to 1 minute, three or four times a day, so that energy can come gushing into our being, flushing out toxins and help us realign ourselves to our true purpose on this planet.

If one cannot do this, perch into naturalness. When we behave unnaturally, it saps our energy. When in natural state, there is clarity about what traits are still there and which ones need to be overcome to blossom into a true child of Nature, forever ready to carry forth her designated tasks. In this process, we need to surmount our shortcomings and enhance our strengths. Nature has made everyone unique and each one of us has a special role to play in the divine design. Being human, we have to experience all emotions and none of them are to be negated. The popular view that emotions are to be suppressed or overcome is not right. Rather, emotions are beautiful expressions of naturalness and only need to be channelised.

When experiencing any anger, irritation or disturbance inside, realise that all of it is energy and immediately use it as a trigger to accomplish some tasks. Channelise this energy by doing some work besides the routine jobs, like arranging things, cleaning, writing or doing something creative.

This is also therapeutic. Many a times I have noticed that when I am really disturbed by what someone said or did, I start cleaning my cupboards and organising shelves, and invariably, come across things that were missing since long, or reminded of somethings I was meant to do but had forgotten. When emotions are treated like tools, they empower, guide and assist in releasing our sub-conscious.

It is amazing that everything lies within us. If we start using our energy wisely, instead of dissipating it in vyarth, meaningless activities, indulgences and conversations, a lot can be achieved.

So, regardless of the feelings that arise within – that of anger or irritation or love, use this thrust of energy constructively. View it like a blessing from the Divine. This energy has come for our uthaan – progress, thus reducing some imperfections or opening a new direction. A very gross example is that of the urge to relieve oneself. It is known as 'nature's call'. This too is Nature's call, the real call. But we misuse it, either indulge in pity that we still are not able to control our emotions or get busy with action-reaction or take it as a shelter for being inactive and indolence.

Finally, everything filters down to one thing – surrender. Be in surrender. If we are truly working on ourselves and are in surrender, we know that whatever is happening is for our betterment, to remind us of something, or to cleanse our subconscious, is not without purpose. In nature, even a storm does not come without a reason. Sometimes it comes to clean the shores, to help cut karmas of some people or create new place.

As a growing tree has energy. The gardener channelises energy by pruning its branches and tying them in some shape so that the tree gets a beautiful appearance. When he cuts and prunes a plant, he is not killing it or cutting down its energy; instead, once pruned, we soon see another branch growing just below the place from where the branch was cut. We too are like that. Nature prunes us by giving impediments in our path. We have to make the choice to pick options that helps us grow, transform and evolve. There is no place for analysing and berating the situation as these deplete energy and flow of new thoughts. The best is to be peaceful, detached, objective and concentrate on doing our best under the circumstances.

The real purpose of energy is to create a congenial atmosphere for peaceful co-existence and humanitarian services. This energy is to be utilised for expansion, for connecting to the universal consciousness which provides new thoughts and messages for future growth. This pure omnipotent and omnipresent energy must be utilised for attaining gyan or knowledge because the Universe does not have any knowledge it only has energies which carry or relay this knowledge. The thoughts and gyan of the evolved souls resides there in the form of energy and we have to understand this mechanism so that we can tap into this vast ocean of unending energies! When a direct connection with the pure energy source is established the mind stops interfering; then all the forces descend according to the time requirement. Whatever chore is done, be it cooking or cleaning, or gardening, it will be beautiful and soulful, pure energy will touch all around to make the environment vibrate with positivity and gaiety.

ॐ

Chapter 21

THE ANGEL AND THREE LAUGHS

Total surrender to the Almighty is the highest form of bhakti. It stands for accepting every situation as a gift or prasad from God. It means living every moment to perfection by using all our mental, physical and spiritual potential to the maximum. Spirituality means doing things in the right spirit and with complete faith. No situation is frivolous or insignificant because it always contains a hidden message.

There are no flaws in the Divine's design, this is what we all must be aware of just like one dev-doot, or angel, did when he was banished from the heaven to lead a life as a cobbler to make him realise the consequence of questioning the wisdom of the Almighty. This angel had become so evolved spiritually that he was just one step away from becoming one with the Supreme. Pointing to a young woman on Earth, God asked him to take away her soul as it was time for her to die. When the angel reached the woman's house, he witnessed a heart-rending scene. Dressed in rags, the woman was cradling a three-month-old baby in her arms and was trying to pacify her two other children, aged two and four, who were crying with hunger. All looked malnourished and pale. There was not a morsel in the house. The woman had lost her husband, their sole breadwinner, a few months ago. With three little children to take care, she was unable to make ends meet. Now she was running high fever and was wondering what was to become of her and her children.

The sight of the poor family living in such trying circumstances, brought tears to the angel's eyes. He could not be so unkind and deprive the helpless kids of their only living parent! His compassion and benevolence got the better of him so he decided to return to the heaven empty handed.

His disobedience earned him the Almighty's displeasure. Since every act of the divine is guided by divine love and benevolence, God decided to make him realise his folly of interfering with the Supreme Law or design by banishing him to Earth for a lifetime as a cobbler. The only way he could return and be with the Almighty once again was by laughing at his plight three times.

Thus the angel was born on Earth into a family of cobblers. He grew up beating smelly hides into smooth leather to make footwear. One day as he sat making footwear, the irony of it all dawned on him and he laughed at his situation – once a dev-doot, God's chosen one, was now on Earth working with animal skins, making footwear for mortals. Anyway, instead of whining, the dev-doot accepted his situation and continued leading his life in total surrender to the Almighty, giving his whole being to whatever work that came in front of him, whether it was beating leather into shape or making footwear.

Soon he became so good at his work that his masters and customers started praising his work. And one day he was asked to make shoes for none other than the king himself! The angel put his mind, heart and soul into his work and before he could realise, he had created the most beautiful pair of chappals ever. But his masters were livid with him for being so careless, wasting raw material and time on a pair of chappals instead of the shoes that the king's men had ordered.

Soon they arrived but much to everybody's surprise, the king's men asked for a pair of chappals instead of shoes. The king had just died, and they wanted chappals to the fit the corpse before it could be cremated. It was a ritual in those days that the body of the king was adorned with chappals rather than shoes on his final journey. The dev-doot was speechless. Nothing seemed frivolous or meaningless in the Almighty's scheme of things, he thought and laughed to himself the second time.

As days passed by, the angel became increasingly well known for his fabulous footwear. One day, a rich elderly lady escorting three pretty girls came to his shop to place a huge order for fancy footwear for the girls as they were all of marriageable age. When the angel asked her whether the girls were her daughters, the lady shook her head and replied that she was a rich businessman's wife but could never have any children. But one day her neighbours told her about three helpless orphans who lost their parents. She felt the Almighty had answered her prayers and she adopted the three kids. The lady was in fact talking about the same children whose mother the Almighty had once ordered him to take away!

Marvelling at the Divine's design, the angel laughed to himself the third time. It was all about surrender and accepting every situation as a gift from God, to be lived through with all our potential. He had been banished to Earth in the first place because he had failed to do so, but later he got the opportunities to laugh his way out of this human life because of his surrender. His life's mission was now complete. He was ready to leave for his heavenly abode where the Almighty was waiting for him with open arms. He knew it well that now he would be with the Supreme forever. He had learnt the ultimate message meant for all humans on Earth that the only way to cut our Karmic Cycle, the cycle of birth and death, for total liberation and merging with the Supreme is to perform every given act may it be in thought, word or deed as an offering to the Lord in total surrender, without doubting or questioning the purpose behind it. This is true realisation. This is the essence of life.

৪৩

TRANSFORM NEGATIVE ENERGY AND DECLUTTER THE SUBCONSCIOUS

To get creative and progressive, start with emptying the subconscious. Only then new fresh ideas will surface. And the best way to do this is by writing and maintaining a daily journal.

Why should we write every day?

To declutter the subconscious, if the subconscious is not emptied, there will be no inner and outer growth.

How to know that the subconscious is full and not empty?

When no new thoughts are arising, no new creative ideas are surfacing, when individuality that you have been bestowed with is not flourishing, when life is moving along a horizontal plane, when flashes of depression are recurring and you are not touching vertical heights in the chosen field of work, know that the subconscious is cluttered.

To ensure that students see and understand with clarity what is written on the blackboard, the teacher has to wipe it clean at the start of a new class. Writing anything on a blackboard already full of chalk marks is a futile exercise. For new ideas to emerge for growth, letting go of the subconscious mess is essential.

All progressive people maintained journals. They penned down their thought process and feelings to have clarity for their path of evolution.

Any other way to empty the subconscious?

There is no better way to declutter the subconscious than writing a daily journal for working on own self. Be your own therapist.

What are the other benefits of journal writing?

Journal writing enables us to know the self. It helps in establishing continuity of thoughts. It makes one centred and it helps in developing the capacity of chintan mannan, contemplating and pondering. It is purification of human mechanism to make one spontaneous.

Many people recommend it, in fact, journal writing used to be part of summer holidays homework too, but being forced to write sometimes puts you off writing all together.

Write whatever arises in the heart — mann and is felt truthfully sincerely without applying too much of the mind.

Some say that we should only write about good things that happened and not about the negative things.

When the mind is used to write only the good things that happened or only that which was or is disturbing, it is essentially the calculative mind's outpouring. The whole idea of journal writing is to empty oneself and realise the truth to be fresh and to welcome the new day with renewed strength. Gratitude will come automatically when you start working on yourself and see its results, feel lighter and confident.

It is not by writing positive things that you will start feeling positive. It is the other way around. While working on the self truly and experiencing the goodness of it naturally you are filled with positivity and gratitude. Then the aura too exudes that. Gratefulness should emerge from within. Journal writing is part of refining your being.

Some people recommend that you write when angry or disturbed. What is the best time to write?

Writing when you are angry or disturbed is a way of releasing the thrust of emotions within. It is for getting little peace and to be comfortable with yourself.

Empty the subconscious anytime when you are tranquil and peaceful. Write down or draw whatever feelings and thoughts that surface. Write till you feel you have poured out everything arising within truthfully.

Diary writing should be like a prayer. Pray and be peaceful. Sit comfortably and write.

Divide the day's page into two parts: things to do and things that flash in dhyan. Writing only what you did or want to do through the day is not enough, also write about your dhyan and thinking pattern, for balancing both the important aspects of human life – worldly and spiritual.

By working on yourself sincerely truthfully and with perseverance you will spontaneously get the messages directives and assistance for further evolution according to your capacity, individuality and the requirement of time.

☯

Chapter 23

LONELY? WRITE A JOURNAL

My diaries are examples of channelising emotional energies into something constructive; from this realisation dawned those Supreme gives sufferings to wake us up, and not because he inclines to trouble us."

Many of us want to become better human beings yet are unaware of how to go about it. Even after best efforts, stubborn habits and reactions hamper the evolutionary path. For self-realisation the importance of de-cluttering the subconscious has to be realised. It has to be emptied to be able to connect and receive the messages essential for growth and full blossoming of life.

The most important tool for unwinding the self is to maintain a journal. Write and pour out everything from the deepest core of the being. Do not judge the choice of words and quality of the expression, instead just let it flow.

This way the heaviness is reduced and the subconscious becomes lighter. Clearing the subconscious weakens the 'gravities' and propels us towards a productive and progressive life.

One should write without inhibitions to pour one's heart out. It should be prolific, as if done on auto pilot. Slowly as one gets used to this form of expression, it becomes cathartic and helps to reduce mental clutter also. This may develop into trans-writing where fresh thoughts messages and directives start to pour to add newness to life along with spiritual growth.

Sometimes doodles and other images might surface. These too have a deep connect with the subconscious and represent hidden fears guilts and desires. Let them manifest without attaching any thoughts like 'this is not good or what use is this.' The whole process when done religiously becomes extremely enjoyable and addictive.

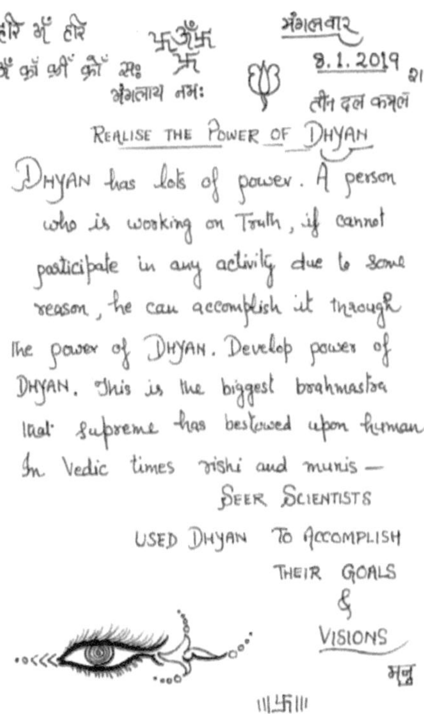

For those connecting to consciousness through Pranam movement, the page of the journal has a specific format. Received in dhyan through years of sadhna by Meena Om, Pranam's founder, each and every aspect of the page has a deep spiritual significance.

It begins by drawing Om flanked by three satiyas (the symbol of Ganeshji) on the top centre of the page. Om represents the primordial sound to connect with whole cosmos. The satiya symbol on three sides around it signifies the prayer, 'may auspicious energies come towards us from all directions and nothing negative touches our being' while remaining connected with the supreme force through Om, much like the connection established through the crown of the head with Supreme Consciousness.

Beneath this 'pranam' is written. Pranam means 'expansion of the soul with humility' and is also a salutation. It is different from namaste which means 'I bow to the divinity within you.'

On the left side of the page is the mantra Hari Om Hari invoking perseverance and perfection – Shri Vishnu. By chanting this mantra we offer ourselves in surrender to become mediums of divine will to live every moment with perfection and to the best of our mental physical and spiritual capacities. The sound vibrations that emanate from chanting Hari Om Hari is spontaneous pranayam which expels mental emotional and physical toxins and brings in fresh energy.

Below this, is the name of the day and its mantra. Each day of the week has a specific energy hence igniting and connecting to it helps in undertaken tasks. The mantra carries the vibrations to connect to the power and energies of that particular day.

On the top right corner of the page is the date and its digits are added up to a single number that is 12.12.2012 add up to 11=2. Hence this number needs to be kept in dhyan through the day. Anything that involves even numbers and its multiples will have a special place on this day. Odd numbers and their multiples are relevant on odd count days. This is based on scientific principles of numerology. Nature and the Universe have an accurate time cycle. It is not a coincidence that Monday is 'Moon day' and Sunday is 'Sun day.' Besides the fact that there are seven colours, seven days of the week, seven seas, seven notes of music and octaves etc.

Adjacent to this is drawn a lotus with petals corresponding to the aggregate date count. The lotus represents detachment purity beauty and grace. The same should descend into my being, draw with this feel. The number of petals drawn act as a reminder of the qualities that are to be nurtured on that day.

These are subtle ways to connect to the energies and be peaceful and centred. Once this system is understood and realised, it helps in unfolding many secrets of the Universe and human existence.

Then the page is broadly divided into two sections — one which states the 'dhyan or thought of the day' and the other 'things to do.'

The dhyan for the day is that which flashes as a thought for refinement of one's being or some past incident that may be there deep in the subconscious. This could be a simple affirmation like – 'today I will not lie' – that needs to be kept in mind as sadhna. The second column of 'things to do' is self-explanatory and clearly delineates the tasks designated for the day.

Well documented events and thoughts help us realise our strengths and weaknesses. Reflecting upon past events at a later date helps us see things in a broader perspective. In life, there are moments of déjà vu. These occur because Nature wants us to approach them differently with a refined self. Continuity of thoughts, deeds and growth is possible by the self-analysis that happens through journal writing. Self-analysis is different from being judgemental toward oneself. One is objective and liberating while the other is subjective and limiting. All these nuances surface through this truly magical method of working on the self. This process needs to become an integral part of uncoiling and learning to know oneself.

Writing a journal thus is a complete act of prayer starting with an invocation followed by release confession meditation and dhyan and putting the pearl of wisdom reaped into practice in daily life.

ॐ

Chapter 24

LONELINESS IS LOVELY

Loneliness is the time for the realisation of your true self – the real being.

Loneliness is a treasure. When circumstances or fate leave us alone that is the time to peep deep into the self to discover hidden treasures. Engrossed in worldly relationships and so-called happiness or sensual pleasures, we fail to tap into our innate capacities and special individuality.

Being alone is Nature's way to create the milieu to address the dormant potential lying inside as a seed. Instead of feeling forlorn and abandoned, it should be taken positively and utilised for growth. The energy created by sadness or grief too can be diverted, pouring out one's emotions into creativity. Out of deep pain arises greater sensitivity to live life more meaningfully.

Have faith that Supreme has endowed everyone with some special talent that needs flourishing. One can write, read, sing and do gardening, arts, crafts or take up other pursuits.

This sensitivity can be utilised to understand other humans too. Nature never leaves anyone bereaved; deprivation is her way to show humans the path to liberation... freedom to love all, to be concerned, to be able to create harmony and bliss. It is not what we go through but what we learn through it that adds dimensions to our personality... just as gold must be tempered in the fire to make it shine. For liberation too we need to pass through trials and tribulation to realise the true value of life. Liberation means being physically, mentally, emotionally sufficient rather than depending upon the help of others or wallowing in self-pity.

If choosing to be alone on the journey for liberation, Supreme Consciousness guides and gives strength to such a human. This is the power of a true sankalp, truthful determination. Besides this there should also be a yearning desire and the fortitude to work on the self.

Instead of assuming loneliness, being alone to be a curse, turn it into blissful solitude to realise the true self. The Supreme bestows loneliness on us to provide us with an opportunity to search for our real self and get connected to the ultimate source of love and joy.

In all pressing circumstances, it is the faith which carries us through, faith in the mechanism of Nature; faith that nothing is frivolous in the Supreme design, faith that we have to sail through every situation with grace and peace; that we are born alone with the inherent capacity for survival and evolution.

The seed of divinity in all is always yearning to sprout and blossom. And this happens during loneliness, tranquillity and solitude. That is why loneliness is lovely. Just make a voluntary choice to devote some time and space for personal growth and evolution.

In loneliness, one can hear the sounds of true harmony, rhythm and perfection of the Universal mechanism.

Use loneliness to find something new or develop a hobby that engrosses the whole being. It may be reading, painting, gardening, music or writing etc. While doing this one might find a like-minded human, a friend or a co-traveller who is of the same mental frequency to enhance the journey of life.

Chapter 25

INNERMOST INNOCENCE: BEAUTY OF INNER BEAUTY

Love is God

God is Love

Love knows no label

Love needs no stamp

Love needs no definition

I am a loner

I was a loner

I will be a LONER

I am alone and I love it most

I am a lover

Lover just lover

Thou live in this body

My only possession my tranquillity

I me myself my soul and my tranquillity

We are five

MY FIVE ELEMENTS

Yes I am alone

But I am not lonely

I am not lonely because my love says

I AM LOVELY

೮೦೮೩

Chapter 26

DO YOU WANT A FRIEND?

Many people complain that – 'I am lonely because I don't have any friends', or they cry – 'No one loves me, people around me don't care about me.' This desire for companionship is natural and normal, but the mind starts to read into relationships, attaches expectations and becomes judgmental that cause grief. In life we meet scores of people, some we call our friends others are mere acquaintances, and we always wonder why certain relationships went sour, or why our 'dear' friends became indifferent. Let me share the reason.

In Bharatiye culture, like many other aspects of life and relationships, there are subtleties in friendship too, which need to be understood. There are many vernacular words for a friend - Dost, mitr, bandhu, sakha – but these are not synonyms. They represent different relationships within the larger ambit of friendship. There are subtle yet vast differences between them. Most people make a friend – mitr or dost and face problems later, because a mitr can be a user – energy sucker or be manipulative.

Yes, there is companionship between the two, they spend time together and become habitual of each other, but this mitr bhav can fluctuate at any point.

Aspire to become a sakha, which is different from being a mitr or dost. A sakha or a 'soul friend' always has badappan, large-heartedness and magnanimity. He is forgiving, always thinks of our welfare even if we behave angrily, be curt or rude, he never looks down at us, or leaves us. Mitrs or friends can be selfish and abandon us, sometimes when we need them the most! Usually, a mitr gets in touch with us to feel good, for a change of mood, or time pass.

Sudama was Krishna's mitr, he was never a sakha. Arjun too could not be a sakha to Krishn because after the Mahabharat got over, he got a little detached and was busy with his own kith and kin. But Krishna never left his sakha bhav. He was always a sakha to everyone.

Till friendship does not turn into sakha bhav, it should be treated as any other worldly relationship and should not be depended upon too much. Most of the time we think that when in friendship, we must sacrifice for a friend, he is everything for us, we love each other, but sooner or later we stumble in this relationship, and intensity fluctuates.

Sakha is a true well-wisher, benefactor, the intensity of connection never gets snaped whether he meets or not. He acts like a teacher, father, mother, sister, brother all rolled into one, a real companion without any selfish motives, never harbours any grudge if someone does not look upon him as something special.

A mitr can be a turn coat. If there is some altercation between two fast friends they can even turn into biggest enemies. In friendships there are expectations, in sakha bhav there are no expectations. In every condition, a sakha only sees kalyan, welfare of all his associates.

Sakha bhav is imbued with karuna, compassion, no triviality, truthfulness, and is closer to the higher self. Right from the beginning, children should be taught the difference between friendship and sakha bhav. Encourage them to be sakha to each other. Be friends, have fun but also know that when the same friend tries to use or encourages them to do undesirable things, he is not their sakha nor a true friend. The one who is not ready to listen to virtuous things is not a nice human being.

There is another kind of acquaintance, called Bandhu. There is not much bondage in being a bandhu. A bandhu is a person who thinks alike. At every point in life, we meet such people who resonate with our mental frequency become our bandhus, walk along with us for a while till time do us apart. We often don't have any complaints or grudges against them. But problems arise when we become mitr – friends, because animosity and bitterness drop in when their views, goals change.

Friendship is related to chakras and puts you in 'chakkar' – rigmarole. People who are functioning through or are at the same chakras are drawn to each other, for example, one is active through heart chakra and so is the other, both will be drawn to each other, but the moment ones energy shifts to heart chakra and the other's to hara – swadhishthan chakra or a higher chakra, they are bound to fall apart.

Keep a watch, are you harbouring some expectation from someone, are you thinking of treating a person well so that he can be of some use to you? If you are working on yourself and are truthful, then help will come to you somehow from any source. No need to be calculative or please them to build contacts. In this way you will make more mistakes, you may leave the path of truth, interfere in other's karmas and get caught up in a karma cycles.

Parents cannot be a sakhas, because they might at some point harbour an expectation from their children, that their children will take care of them in old age. In some cases parents and children may part their ways.

A Sakha is a benefactor, he loves all equally and is without any ulterior motive. He never deters from this even if you don't meet for long periods or harbours pangs of separation. If someone withdraws from a sakha, he will take it in its own stride and when that person comes back again he will receive him with same sakha bhav. Sakha is a manifestation of pure consciousness with only one feel – welfare of all.

॰ॐ॰

Chapter 27

TOWARDS THE HIGHER SELF

O Lord give me the strength

To Mother all the wants of others

A sakha in need

A constant mentor

And co-traveller in tranquillity

Eradicating all agonies

With a smile

Scattering the clouds of grief

Gloom and depression

Caring Always

Pointing at the eternal truth

To be firm dedicated

Sincere in driving human

Towards highest self

This is my Karm

This is Truth

৪৩৪৪

Chapter 28

OVERCOMING FEAR AND REGRET

Loneliness often arise when we have a fear of being left alone, while alienation is caused when we move away from situations out of insecurity, doubts, lack of confidence and even regrets.

Both fear and regret can be circumvented to some extent by addressing the cause and working on the self.

Accept that you are fearful, then meditate or contemplate over what you are afraid of. Find the cause of fear, enlarge it to the biggest, most fierce state and then offer it to Supreme – asserting 'I am out of it now, what is good for me will surely happen.'

Suppose you are afraid of falling and getting hurt, enlarge that fear, imagine the worst thing in detail and visualise that scenario – for example falling, having an accident so severe that could lead to even death!

Confront it and reason it out: Life and death are not in our hands. Everything is Divine will, so why be scared, instil the assertion, "I will go through everything, whatever happens, with ease peace and grace. Meanwhile, let me celebrate life, the best gift bestowed upon me by Supreme." Constant jap of any mantra that one relates to also helps.

Fear attracts more fear, mishaps and accidents. It has to be faced and braved by strong will, not to be negated or set aside for it will become a part of the subconscious mind. Being fearful also is a sign of taking shelter of the fear for being inactive. Be honest to yourself, introspect, work on yourself and be free from this overbearing shortfall.

ALIENATION AND OVERCOMING REGRETS

A shift in the thought process is required to heal oneself. In life, everything is a choice of our inner magnate. The Supreme has bestowed us with the power to change the course of our life, we only need to believe and have faith in it. Regrets lead to guilt, which is one of the weight on our soul and this attracts misfortune that retards our progress.

Five things we often regret:

1. I did not have the courage to live a life true to myself.

2. I did not resist the assaults on my self-respect or say no to injustice to my being.

3. I did not express my feelings.

4. I am losing touch with people who once loved and cared for me.

5. I don't allow myself to be happier by being out of guilt and fear.

Be fearless and follow the path of truth love karm and light.

It is our inner magnetism that attracts people and situations into our lives to teach us lessons required for growth and transformation. This is the perfect universal mechanism for evolution but the human wants to have his own way due to ego, security of his comfort zone or to avoid working on himself, creating a vicious karma cycle.

Gravities or situations that pull one down or hinder progress come to everyone who is on the path of growth and is trying to carve out a life according to his inner call. So why bother about others who spread negativity. They are tuned to behave in a certain manner and thus to go through their own karmas. Pray for them. Just be centred in your own resolve and truth, ready to face everything that comes as a test to propel you towards growth glory and grace.

OVERCOMING REGRETS

It is a law of Nature – *Param Bodhi*, Supreme Intelligence always tests us. After going through these trials with all our might, one is bestowed with the bliss of spiritual highs and joyous 'aha' moments. So just have faith – the Supreme never tests one beyond one's capacities, only prepares us for some higher cause and the realisation of the absolute Truth. Striking a balance between Nature and one's own nature, and making life a celebration by being content, peaceful and joyful on all planes is a requirement of Nature's law.

CONTRACTION AND DILATION

Contraction-dilation is a law of Nature for moving ahead, like the gait of an earthworm. Contraction is detachment from the outer world; it means to be centred in the inner self. This is the time for self-introspection as well as being firm in our personal resolves, unaffected by the chaos around. Some assume this 'contraction' time as loneliness and not manage to get the best message or directive out of it. This state helps in conserving energy for our next flight, so we can thrust back into the world with renewed focus, energy and strength.

Dilation is a conscious expansion, spreading out to feel one with the whole atmosphere and creation, moving along with it for the progression of life. It happens when the being is replete with strength of inner will, vision and courage to make it manifest. In this state, energy needs to be conserved and applied to only those tasks that assist in our growth and fulfilment of our resolves. If care is not taken, then we feel depleted and the goal is not achieved. Then again one needs to go back into the contraction phase to recoup and arise.

Both of these are perfectly normal states of being and should not be considered otherwise.

ॐ

Chapter 29

HAVE THE COURAGE TO CHANGE

Loneliness arises when we resist change. Change is constant, change is inevitable – all evolved masters and ancient scriptures state this and yet we are scared of change.

Writers of the scriptures were truthfully connected to Nature and its truth. Everyone knows Nature is ever-evolving, growing, changing every nano second. We are also products of Nature, therefore, have to change like her. Our problem is that all the time we try hard to make our lives convenient, comfortable, manageable so as to toil less – to the extent that unknowingly life becomes monotonous. To kill monotony and boredom we indulge in outward distractions such as shopping, clubbing or partying thus losing precious time and energy. All the time we search for ways to remain in some comfort zone or a cocoon that we have created so diligently for ourselves. Never pondering and preparing for the change that might come in unwarranted ways to jolt us out of our inertia. The ones who have not prepared for exams get scared of them.

The whole creation is based on contradictory things, only balance is required. Monotony is always followed by some twist or change. One grows by sailing through it, with ease peace and grace or succumbs to depression or diseases.

What is the best way to manage change? Should we be nonchalant about it or welcome it?

The word 'managing' is outcome of ego and sense of 'doer-ship' – that one can manage. It is not to be managed but lived with all might. Welcome it, sky is the limit for human capacity. Capacities become capabilities and sensitivities become sensibilities with tests of time.

That all-loving Supreme Intelligence never thrusts hardships that are beyond our handling. The problem is with our mind that wants change according to its own design. But the change that propels us towards growth is always according to Divine's design. Be receptive and welcome this Supreme grace.

It is true that it becomes part of our nature to resent change. Let me ask you, are you always sure of your own chalked out plans. As the saying goes, 'Man proposes, God disposes'. Change tries all our faculties – of pondering over things, concentration, physical fitness to act accordingly, exploring unknown dimensions, to be along with time, and be confident and sure of ourselves. However, we are mostly unprepared and unwilling to do sadhana with perseverance to come out with our own answers and wisdom lying deep within, wisdom that needs to surface to remind us of our special individuality waiting to blossom through constant change.

What should we keep in mind at mental, physical and soul levels to address change?

The most important thing is peace and tranquillity. Not getting affected too much by situations, people and even climates; sailing through everything with open mind and with ease, peace, and grace tunes our system to deal with everything according to this golden rule that has to get embedded in our system.

Mind chattering along with nurturing fears, guilts or doubts can cloud our minds. Save energy from every frivolous thing to get messages and directives from inside. Actually, we are over-loaded with information, answers, knowledge from books, media, friends or even from mentors. It is much better to have little pearls of knowledge and few answers and work on these sincerely by living and experiencing to arrive at your own answers and decisions, to enjoy new-found confidence, and gyan – that is not mere knowledge or information.

In what way is change related to growth?

See and observe a small plant closely. It changes its shape, size, and even colour daily on the way to full blossoming. If it does not change and grow, it perishes. Change brings newness. When your aura is transformed by going through changes with your inner strength, and power of sankalp to ride every wave; it can transfer the thought to others also to change and grow.

Growth is joy of life, there is no stagnancy, no tension, no depression in growth. You are energetic always, clarity dawns about things, people, situations and even life. There are so many things we fear for, losing wealth and youth, mishaps and death. One of the greatest fears is that of being left behind time, for this, one goes on accumulating latest clothes, jewellery, furniture and so many things but we hardly work on our inner self or on the happenings around us and in the world. Work on the self to prepare for change that will propel you towards growth – transformation and evolution.

How to always be on the path of progress?

Always follow the path of truth, love, karm, and light. Eternal, true dharm based on the laws of Nature and perfect universal mechanism. Be Brahma Vishnu Mahesh – symbolically – create perfect and destroy something daily from outside and inside. Outside, plant, paint, write, clean, declutter, make new arrangement or even cook something new daily. Try to perfect it. Get rid of what is not required. Do same for internal spaces. Think something new daily, new thoughts, ideas that gives flight to imagination. Expanding your limitations mentally, do pruning and elimination of old habits, tunings, preconceived notions about people, situations, things and social, religious or spiritual norms – fill in newness. Work on yourself for growth, to be prepared for every situation.

Ego and non-performance; being judgemental about everything – people, situations and systems – and wasting time on frivolous things, are some of the hurdles on the path of progress.

Either learn or teach something. Let there not be single moment when you are not creating, perfecting and destroying something – that is undesirable for growth – or poses hurdles to new pastures for further transformation and evolution.

How to know that we are evolving?

When you are on the path of growth, all questions, doubts, dualities, resentments, preconceived notions, and anger starts to subside. Depression and gloom evaporate. You look forward to new happenings, messages and directives knowledge – gyan to enhance your spirits and to move on – and feel the happiness, joy and peace within yourself.

Your aura spreads happiness and positivity all around. You are comfortable in every situation, climate and atmosphere. There are no complaints, no snarling, no sulking.

You enjoy and reap the benefits of the answers and knowledge gained from every source, from daily activities and even from own thinking process. You feel in sync with everything, the whole creation, feel oneness, newness to relish the human existence.

↾⇀

Chapter 30

MANTRA FOR EVOLUTION: ARPAN TARPAN SAMARPAN

Our breath is like a conveyor belt. It carries into the Universe our thoughts, words, actions, and intent. And draws to us energy from the Universe for creative living and to fulfil our purpose of existence.

Whatever we do, has to be like arpan – an offering to the Divine. This way one does not get tied to the karm – action, that is, get caught in karma, the cause-and-effect cycle of the action.

Since everything we do is to be like an offering, can we offer maligned things, complaints, criticism, abuses to the Divine?

No. Whatever we throw into the Universe via the breath, comes back to us manifolds; this is true for pious thoughts as well as abusive ones. So, since everything is prasad from the Divine, we need to be careful that we are offering only the best – perfect action, best thoughts, and right speech.

For all the existing burdens of the soul, imperfections of the body, polluted thoughts of the mind, we should do tarpan. Like we do tarpan for our ancestors, wishing them well for their journey ahead and delinking ourselves from them, as part of the final rituals. Whenever any troubling thought arises, past incidents surface in the mind, whenever realisation dawns that you have acquired some bad habits or are nurturing some vices, do their tarpan. Visualise that you are releasing them into the Universe, offering them to the Divine for recycling, and are getting cleansed of them.

There is no better way to cleanse your subconscious mind than tarpan. Continue doing this repeatedly until the bothersome thoughts stop surfacing or troubling.

For the situations and people that come in front to you, be in samarpan, in surrender to the Divine's will. No complaining or brooding.

Know that everything, situation or people that come, is meant to cut our past karm; take us forward; help us evolve further spiritually; indicate the path ahead, illuminate our mann and buddhi - mind and intellect; awaken us from Sushupti – slumbering state; and show us what karm to give up and which to continue performing.

Every action that we are supposed to perform, is to be done to the best of one's abilities and capacities.

The Divine exists in each and every particle. Truth is present in each and every molecule. The one who does the sadhana of

Truth, is truthful in his words, thoughts and deeds, Satyeshwar – Truth as Supreme Entity – uses that person's ability to absorb the truth and be a medium to reveal his divine Swaroop, form. This becomes the source of courage and energy for all his future endeavours and illuminates his life's path ahead.

We slot all happenings in our life as good or bad and then suffer. If we live each one of them to the fullest, go through them with all our abilities and capabilities, wholeheartedly, derive the gyan hidden in them, learn from them, we will never suffer or stagnate. We will always stay gatimaan, on the move.

But by chewing like cud the incidents that have happened, we only waste our time, sometimes years. We stall our progress. So, 'arpan, tarpan and samarpan', is the mantra to evolve and glow.

ॐ

Chapter 31

ENJOY THE JOURNEY OF LIFE

It is much better to go on walking steadily, rather than go through a steep rise and a deep fall. In Hindi there are sayings, 'Na sawan harey na bhado sukhey' – neither green in the rainy season, nor dry in autumn. There is a deep message hidden in this. If we have a chosen path, be firm, steady, rejoice and live every moment, slowly and constantly with perseverance. Do not get waivered by achievements or downfalls. When in a hurry to achieve something – downfall is inevitable. Searching for shortcuts, we might get delayed or caught up in some cobweb.

Plants, trees all take their own time to blossom slowly and steadily.

'Naam bhajey so sukh dukh chhutey' - chant the Divine's name and get detached from all pleasures and pain. Carry on walking, moving away from sukha and dukha to make anand, bliss to happen.

Mostly people are in a hurry, looking out for some miracles for personal gain. Engrossed in their own motives they are not seeking any spiritual evolution, not even desiring or aspiring to contribute anything for the growth of humanity, absolutely self-centred.

Stop being anxious about the path and the destination. Instead, perform karm, dutiful action, with full dedication, wisdom; using mental and physical capacities to the maximum. Accept that every thought that has surfaced within has emerged from the Divine, to enhance our path. Get high on the experience of performing karm in surrender to the divine will... do not crib, 'if this happens, then I will do that.' This is the only way to bliss. Who knows what the result might be. It might be different from what was envisioned. Perhaps it might be more beneficial, conducive for evolution. So wholeheartedly, do the karm and offer it to Prabhu, the Supreme Entity.

Precious life should not be wasted by over thinking. Whatever transpired was for the best, whatever is happening is also fine, and will be all right in the future too, this is the only gist. Only anand is anandayi – only bliss is blissful. The moolmantra, key mantra is to live every moment fully, in which there lies the welfare of all.

Find amusement in every moment of life and be in gratitude that the body and its systems are in order working fine. Constantly remembering the Divine. Go on working without getting affected or disturbed by great upheavals. These take their own time to pass...so work hard, meditate, take care of the health to keep up energy levels. The greatest problem is the mind and its thinking pattern – 'if this happens then we will do that.' Shri Krishn states in Geeta, that one must have a clear goal, perform consistent karm -actions, with absolute surrender. Maintaining absolute faith in the Divine and remembering that upheavals happen to test our resilience for our growth and evolution.

The word Upheaval itself is self-explanatory, up and heave, i.e. to lift up. The easiest way to tackle it is to do karm with ease and peace. All doubts and dualities are only mind games, manipulations, calculations or shortcuts. Mind is the greatest culprit that makes everything complicated.

Nature's fury is bound to be unleashed when her creation is malignant with falsehood or imperfection; when it is not of her design, fitting into new growth and evolution.

Awake O human...listen to the call of Time.

May the grace of Supreme descend upon all to be aware and act – do karm, according to the requirement of the time...to impart power of dhyan to listen to Consciousness and have the strength to follow the path of truth, love, karm, and light.

☙❧

Chapter 32

POISED SERENITY

Poised serenity is seed of

Grace and peace

Every gesture and act

Happens as if from

Some higher plane

Outcome of tranquil strength

Facing all happenings with perfect

Ease and peace

Perfect ease & peace

Just witnessing the happenings

But fully conscious and aware

Of everything

Dwelling in the peace

That pervades in all the spaces around

The peace that emerges

From deepest core of divine abode inside

To make soul eternally established in

The truthful domain

Of the ETERNAL

ॐ

Chapter 33

BREATHE WITH AWARENESS

Karm, action is not something external alone. It also involves consistently working on the inner self. The most important aspect of internal karm is to synchronise breathing with awareness. Awareness of every aspect of life, what is happening around us and in the world. Only then both the planes – worldly and spiritual – can be balanced.

Right breathing technique involves aligning the breath with constant sumiran, remembrance, and through it connecting with the Supreme energy that is omnipresent, omnipotent and omniscient.

The cyclical waves of inhaling and exhaling are the medium to transmit thoughts into the Universe. It is common knowledge that when a truthful sankalp resolve, is sent forth, the whole Universe conspires to fulfil it. If we are not aware of our thoughts, we often transmit things that are according to mind's tuning, which is a product of our environment and thinking patterns.

We must be aware of our capacities and our special purpose on Earth. Knowing our thoughts, resolves, what is happening around and within, knowledge one is gaining from media, books, events, people and situations – is awareness. The next step is to synchronise your determination, idea or vision with the rhythm of breathing. Chanting silently along with the breath, any small mantra helps to remember and connect to the supreme energies. Pray for the divine form and divine attributes to descend within the being. Realising this mechanism of creating a link with universal energies is what breathing with awareness means.

Usually while we breathe, our mind runs helter-skelter, thinking of something else. To align with the breath and to bring in the awareness of our true aspirations, practice is needed. Even our outer acts should be coordinated, for example, while cooking the thought must be that the food being cooked is made well and provides nourishment to those who eat it. Similarly, while painting the aspiration should be that viewers feel the bhav, with which it is created. This is regulating breath with awareness and living in the moment. But usually both processes are not in sync. We just go on breathing mechanically and think of something else while performing outward acts. This causes imbalance that creates chaos, confusion and duality within our being.

The purpose of the breath is to energise and refresh. When we are not aware the mind runs amok, it is not in sync with the breath thus it depletes energy. We rarely combine it with enhancing and progressive thoughts. Usually, we indulge in depressing, negative musings, or in criticising and analysing others. The great Indian saint, Kabir, says, 'In every breath, O Supreme, may I never forget thy name.' This reflects bhakti, reverence for the highest entity, Supreme, above us all. A person on the path of gyan knowledge or karm action, must be clear about his thoughts and resolves. Only then will there be a constant consistent connection with the Supreme that empowers to fulfil our resolves. This is what it means to conjoin awareness with the breath.

When awareness sprouts within and we set it aside or start analyzing it, then mind chatter infiltrates and the inner self gets embroiled in the vicious circle of our thinking patterns.

Connecting awareness to the breath means to get empowered for our sankalps resolves, along with getting insights to perform associated actions efficiently. Right energy, messages and directives do not descend if we do not regulate our vision, mission and aspirations with the breath. This is also known as internal karm yog.

There was a time in life when my being was facing a lot of problems. At that time awareness dawned that these have come to teach something, to improve my being, so I should not indulge in any blame game. Connecting this awareness with the breath, I prayed, 'O Supreme, guide me how to come out of these problems. Bestow upon me shakti power and gyan wisdom, to go through this turmoil with ease peace and grace.' Then guidance started pouring in.

While doing worldly tasks do not hold, increase or decrease the pace of the breath that is happening naturally and effortlessly. Our inner gyan knowledge and jagriti good thoughts and awareness should relate to the breath to get enough strength to move ahead, towards growth and transformation in life. Breath should not be just for throwing out air and carbon dioxide into the Universe. We must expel undesirable thoughts along with our breath to empty our subconscious and to get filled with new light.

Breathing with awareness enables us to listen to the Supreme Consciousness and act accordingly. This enhances inner capacities to grow along with the natural process of reformation and evolution. This wonderful act of conscious breathing does miracles to our physical, mental, emotional and spiritual wellness; it provides us with true insights to do right things at the right time.

Breathing does not require any calculation or force. It is a natural process, an involuntary system. One has to ride this natural flow for carving a magnificent pattern and path to get connected to all universal energies, to justify this human existence. Breath is the only mechanism that can connect us with the whole creation, whole and complete -poorn, to experience the bliss of oneness.

Be aware of the truth that the breath is called Pran Vayu – The Universal Life Force – by Vedic seer-scientists. Humans have yet to explore its full potential to be part of the perfect rhythm and harmony of the cosmic design.

We have been bestowed with the most precious thing, the breath – to get connected to the Supreme Entity Mahati Tattve – that runs the whole show.

ॐ

Chapter 34

CONSTANT CONNECTION FOR TRUE REALISATION AND ENLIGHTENMENT

The limitations of the mind is cornering humans to depend more on artificial intelligence and other means to deal with life challenges and the inner restlessness that most are experiencing. However, this is an indication of the transitionary period towards the next steps of evolution, where old tuned or set ways of the mind and behaviour will be a hinderance for inner growth and evolution.

The visible expansion of materialistic mentality on the pretext of globalisation must now be diverted from the external towards true internal spaces. Instead of connecting to consumerist commodities, the linkage of our brain, mind, heart and soul energies must be with a higher power, to know, realise and utilise their real strength for our true purpose of life.

Now there is no escape from understanding the Universal mechanism of connectivity and feel of oneness. The consequences of ignoring this will force Nature to unleash its calamities to corner humans into realising the true meaning of life. Our existence needs to be devoid of ego with focus on inner growth with surrender and gratitude.

For human to evolve, it is essential to maintain a steady, constant and consistent connection with our inner true self and/ or the divine spark within an evolved being. This persistent association and connection helps to realise:

- Detachment from all desires and things which are detrimental for growth, transformation and evolution.
- The feel of synchronicity between our own thoughts, words, deeds and the divine will.
- Compassion, consideration and concern for all matter and being, a natural spontaneous soulful kindness and selflessness; not hypocritical exhibition or flaunting of goodness.
- Elimination of ego, indulgences and attachments.
- Descent of divine guidance and directives for all our endeavours.
- Eagerness to follow laws of nature and cosmic principles.
- Dedication towards spreading the message of Truth, Love, Karm and Light.
- The feel of oneness with the whole creation dawns after absolute renunciation of frivolous things and worldly calculations, manipulations, forcing, insisting, designing.

Renunciation is required for being centred in the true inner being and there is a need for consciously detaching from all expectations, aspirations which can sublimate into a feel of separation. Oneness is the feel where one realises that everything is interconnected. It propels us towards expansion of pure love, that diminishes all conflicts and dualities. To feel oneness, consciousness needs to expand to the state where it merges with the divine Supreme Consciousness – True Yog. Then one becomes absolutely anchored in peace and bliss; true realisation of the supreme entity – Param Tattve dawns.

Enlightenment happens when one achieves the state of non-attachment, devoid of all indulgences, longings, wants and desires. In this absolute awareness our whole being is connected to and directed by the guiding light of Supreme Intelligence.

The one who is doing sadhna, sustained practice to fathom this truth of constant connection, is on the right path, carved by Supreme Intelligence for the next evolutionary step. One must realise the truth of micro differences between every species, acceptability of every situation, event and happening as a medium towards change and transformation, adapting the being for a new era of the next phase of evolution.

Artificial Intelligence, natural disasters and viral pandemics have revealed how much one is interconnected and interdependent on others and outer means for help, strength, support and assistance. In the same manner we all are connected to each other and external energies through our thinking patterns, aspirations, visions, ideas, goals in life. It is time now to realise the potential of this powerful mechanism. A new evolutionary understanding is surfacing of mutual accountability and aspirations to feel connected to all because everyone is a part of that Supreme being and the perfect cosmic pattern.

Natural evolution is propelling humans towards unified thinking, and collective consciousness for the feel of oneness. Every thoughtful human should aspire to do sadhna to be a benign and authentic human. It is time now for survival of reformed ones, because transformation and evolution is speeding up and change is inevitable. That is why humans are indulging fiercely in their own mind sets and acquired traits, good or bad to make it easier for Nature to sieve genuine and refined ones for the quantum leap. There will be physical and mental change in the generations to come. One needs to be very cautious to not be disturbed and interfere with these nature induced transformations. Now we have to work on ourselves to be deserving of the Supreme benevolence and grace.

Essentially all humans have to be out of the field of I, Me and Mine and realise the connection between all matter and being, Nature and the Cosmos that is omnipotent, omniscient and omnipresent. It has no empty space, no void, everything is a part of one whole complete mechanism, process and mosaic, template and layout of the Supreme Design Matrix.

৪৩৫৪

Chapter 35

FAITH MAKES EVERYTHING AUSPICIOUS

Aisa ho badan ki Krishn ka mandir dikhayee de

Aisa ho mann ki Krishn hee Krishn sujhayee de

Let the body be a temple of Krishn

Let the heart reflect only Krishn.....

Know the secret of the conviction of faith... In life, faith is everything. Faith is not another name for blind devotion. To ensure that everything around us is auspicious, we have to become deserving. Only by following the path of truth, love and karm, can we become worthy of God's grace. Even after maintaining faith, some people have complaints and objections regarding the Divine will. Questions like 'why did this happen' start raising their head. This is because having left everything to faith and their belief in God; they start living according to their self-chosen path. What takes prominence is the 'doer-ship' of their conviction that God has to keep everything 'in order' for their good, because of their faith in Him.

Human beings do not have the wisdom to realise the fact that we have to be open and deserving of God's grace when it descends. Because of ignorance caused by falsehood, pride, hypocrisy, selfishness, attachment, egos, etc., the doors of our *mann*, heart, are closed to the divine grace. Open the doors of your heart and see that not only divine grace but divinity itself will flow towards you.

For example, if you face a tiger in a jungle how will you react? Will you start chanting a mantra to dispel fear and enemies. Or will you request the beast to wait so you may go to a temple and consult an astrologer to please the gods to find a remedy for overcoming this dangerous situation.

In such a situation, only three kinds of yog, union with the Divine Consciousness can help. Firstly, if there is pure, poorn, complete, unconditional love in your eyes then, even a ferocious animal will give way to such a saintly person.

Secondly, if you analyse the situation with dhyan, full awareness, wisdom and spontaneity and initiate right conduct at the right time, the dynamics of the situation can be changed to save oneself. This is possible only because of sadhna, incessant dedication of a karm yogi towards dharm, right conduct at the right time.

Thirdly and finally, there is the force of truth. To face truth with absolute fearlessness – knowing the fact that the truth of the moment demands you to become food for an animal, and that it has divine sanction and yet remain unaffected by it. Such complete fearlessness will influence your body language, leading to a miracle. This is the power of satya, truth.

Even if the slightest doubt enters your mind that 'O God, in spite of having complete faith in you, you are showing me this day,' then faith will not work.

So, O human, faith is definitely the ultimate refuge, but, it is only due to the amalgamation of truth, love and karm, that divine grace descends.

Faith is the pride and beauty of humanity, the source of energy and only through truth, love and karm, can the human body become the medium of its descent. This is the greatness of human body, the existence.

Human life is a precious gift, so

Keep open always, the doors of thy heart,

Open all its locks

With the key of faith, truth, love and karm.

This is the essence of life

Its secret revealed by Pranam

This is the Truth.

ॐ

Chapter 36

I AM THE SOUL

I am the soul

I am only a soul

Content, whole and complete in my soulfulness I dwell in the qualities of the soul

Playing with it

Talking to it

Connecting conversing with the soul of others Experiencing that

Engrossed in self-realisation Exuding the qualities of the soul

This body lit by the Supreme

Has become

The light of Supreme's lamp.

Chapter 37

BE A FLOWER OF HUMANITY

Aayi Basant, pala udant.

When Basant comes, spring arrives and the cold evaporates.

The Earth awakens to the loving warmth of the sun and colourful flowers begin to blossom, spread joy, positivity, and fragrance. They hold within their folds deep spiritual messages for humanity.

A flower is a culmination of the beautiful essence of growth; a symbol of consistently working on the self and then offering it to the world. It gives the seed, which represents continuity of the sankalp, resolve of imparting the best of your being.

A flower tells us in silent language that we are perfect creatures, reflection of the divine and by working on ourselves, and taking right nutrients and withstanding the blows of natural calamities and other assaults, we can blossom fully. Flowering fully reflects divinity; it symbolises the journey of life in a very concise manner.

We have to imbibe this gyan. If we leave a seed, a thought behind, it should be according to our individuality, what we have blossomed into with our constant sadhana -consistent practice.

A flower gives food, nourishment, joy of karma to all the insects, butterflies to honeybees… till it lasts. It does not hold on to its benevolence. Similarly, we should work hard, take right nutrients and have the wisdom of what to attract and imbibe for a lasting vision or resolve of spreading joy and light, leaving the essence in seed form that carries on this natural procedure.

A plant perishes but never succumbs to circumstances. It never compromises with its qualities and mission. It knows the highest perfect mechanism of nature, full blossoming of being. Everyone can blossom into perfection, that beauty which reflects divinity, which is beneficial for the whole creation.

Flowers are detached from the feelings of sorrow and joy, offered at the altar in temples and other places of worship, graves, and adorning joyous occasions and that of grief alike. As the Bhagwad Geeta states for a yogi – flowers too are centred in sambuddhi, equanimity and are stithapragya, firmly established in one's truth, providing smiles and solace to everyone.

Being divine, they never reject anyone, unlike people who sometimes view others with disgust and resentment.

When a flower blossoms there are no vehement gestures or clamour. It blossoms for its own joy, according to its own gunas, as per Nature's law, in complete surrender.

The plant knows that it is has to flower, blossom and offer a perfect seed. The seed of joy, happiness, life and medicinal values. One can feel refreshed and energised by the healing aura of flowers.

A seed captures the essence of the flower when it blossoms fully, it would not happen earlier or later than that. Perfect timing and tuning. It represents continuity of the dhyan of the plant, which grows to finally wither away leaving behind its own replica in seed form.

Humans are mostly unaware of the kind of seed – thought – they are leaving behind, being totally engrossed in the worldly mire.

Different flowers have specific significance; lotus represents wisdom and detachment; rose stands for love; sunflower for solar energy; lily for piousness; daisy reflects innocence and hope and marigold symbolises joy.

A flower is a divine reminder to all of us to blossom fully in given life. It only takes the set amount of nutrients essential for its growth. Offer more water to the plant, it will perish but it never takes excess. A stronger plant will stay aloof from excess, absorbing only the amount it needs. When it blossoms fully, it never holds on to it, and surrenders gracefully to withering away. But its aim is always to give a proper seed and attract proper insects for pollination – such is its dhyan. It's true inner core attracts this in surrender and is happy and contented with its own attributes. We are never happy with our qualities because of being tuned by various influences – parents, teachers, and peers. So our mind indulges in doubts and dualities.

We too are flowers of the Supreme, planted on the Earth, but we have created a mess by using too much mind. A flower is a perfect play of energies, colours and fragrance. We too can blossom in whichever field we are in if we imbibe the qualities of a flower and do justice to our existence.

৪৩

AUTHOR PROFILE

Meena Om is a modern-day seer-scientist, practical visionary, and a spiritual mentor. Through a spiritual movement called Pranam, she has been working relentlessly to spread the message of Truth; Love; Karm, right conduct at the right time; and Light, eradication of ignorance wherever prevalent. Besides providing clear, tangible insights into true spirituality, Meena ji exemplifies how original Vedic seer-scientists functioned, manifesting supreme truths by maintaining perfect synchronicity with Nature and the Universal mechanism.

Meena ji's perceptions of Supreme Consciousness, expressed through trans-writing, are manifesting continuously in a flow and are being recorded in a spontaneous and sincere manner. Hidden in these writings is profound wisdom that imparts clarity and intense insights into real spirituality. The subtle and lyrical symmetry of Nature at its macro as well as micro levels is expressed and delivered with ease through her effortless connection with Nature. She even talks about an inner unseen anatomy that contains answers to many scientific conundrums yet to be explored by formal sciences.

Meena Om is a 'de-mystified' mystic, who aspires to ignite minds of genuine seekers to seek, get empowered to listen to the time call and act accordingly for the welfare of all, towards harmonious co-existence.

ॐ